MUSIC AND WORSHIP

GRATEFULLY INSCRIBED

TO

THE MOST REVEREND THE

LORD ARCHBISHOP OF CANTERBURY

MUSIC & WORSHIP

by

WALFORD DAVIES

and

HARVEY GRACE

1935
EYRE AND SPOTTISWOODE
LONDON

MADE AND PRINTED IN GREAT BRITAIN FOR
EYRE AND SPOTTISWOODE (PUBLISHERS), LONDON

AUTHORS' PREFACE

IN 1932 we were jointly deputed by the Cathedral Organists' Association to write a pamphlet on church music, for use in Theological Colleges. We had proceeded only a little way, however, before seeing that the pamphlet must become a book, and that what we had to say on the subject could perhaps be usefully addressed not only to ordinands, but to all who are in any way responsible for and interested in church music.

At that time there came to one of us an urgent request from our publisher for a book for general readers on the whole subject of Music as the Voice of Worship. This, we felt, called us to widen our basis and quicken our efforts to meet a far more general need.

A very considerable army of musicians—chiefly voluntary—is occupied in the provision of music for purposes of public worship. The efficiency of this army is naturally a matter of concern to all who care for the health and reality of corporate worship. The possibility of increase, improvement, and development of that army seems to us to be incalculably great. That its present short-comings are obvious is no matter for regret, for its possibilities are hardly less apparent. Owing to the boon of wireless transmission, a mere chant sung perfectly by some humble choir in a remote part of the country may now be heard by millions. Any little platoon of a choir may thus in a few minutes set a standard of diction and choral ensemble to which every choir in the whole army must try to reach or lose its self-respect.

Church music is like no other music in that a failure to co-ordinate the team into an ensemble as simple and perfect as possible is not only a musical short-coming but also a defeat of the very spirit of worship which the music sets out to serve. The ideals of music in worship are therefore considered here as the most exacting yet most homely concern of all. But the practical applications that are suggested and discussed in this book are particularly addressed to those enthusiasts who somehow feel that, after centuries of splendid achievement and humiliating lapses, church music has arrived at a stage where the call seems to be for a reconsideration of first principles. Our endeavour has been to answer this call, rather than to produce one more addition to the large number of admirable and practical textbooks that already exist.

Collaboration has been as real and complete as we could make it. Most of the chapters were written on a fifty-fifty plan, and the work of each of us has been very freely overhauled by the other.

We offer to our co-workers in church music the

outcome of a long combined experience in no dogmatic spirit. The fact that those experiences have been gained in such widely different spheres of work as village, slum and cathedral churches has made us realize how widely the needs of choirs and congregations must vary in regard to material and methods. But behind all this variety must be the energizing force of unity in aim and principle, and it is mainly upon the latter that we have tried to concentrate in the spirit of earnest inquiry.

W. D.

H. G.

December, 1934.

BIBLIOGRAPHY

THE literature of church music is now so large that a comprehensive list is out of the question. We have therefore confined ourselves to works that are practical and inexpensive, and of which we have personal knowledge. The saving of space enables us to add a few particulars concerning the books.

CHOIR TRAINING

Choirs in Little Churches. The Rev. Stuart Morgan. (Faith Press. Paper, 1s. ; cloth, 2s.)

Written during the author's incumbency of a Sussex village, where the methods described in the book were used with success.

The Organization and Training of Parish Choirs. Francis T. Kennard. (*Musical Opinion* Office. 2s.)

A simple and practical booklet by a parish church organist, based on his experiences with voluntary choirs in poor districts.

The Amateur Choir Trainer. Henry Coleman. (Oxford University Press.)

Dr. Coleman's book is designed primarily for non-professional choir-masters, but its scope and practical character make it valuable for all who are engaged in choral training. It contains chapters on subjects not usually dealt with in works of the kind—"Sight-Reading," "The Boy's Changing Voice," " The Alto Part," " The Organ : Its Use and Abuse," etc.

The Little Choir Book. Thomas Curry. (Novello. 1½d.)

Deals simply with the rudiments of music. The section on chanting is out of date, but the work is still of value, as it deals with a department of knowledge that is too often taken for granted or shirked.

The Dual Notation Course for Sight-singing in Both Notations. L. G. Venables. (Curwen. In four parts, 3d. each. Teachers' edition, 2s. 6d. each).

Part I may be used alone with profit by small parish choirs.

Class Singing. W. G. Whittaker. (Oxford University Press. 6s.)

Though written primarily for use in secondary schools, this work contains much that is of vital importance to all engaged in choral training. The teaching of sight-singing is fully dealt with.

Time and Rhythm Exercises. Walter S. Vale. (Faith Press. 1d.)

An excellent method of combining voice-training with the teaching of time-notation.

Tone Production in the Human Voice. Walter S. Vale. (Faith Press. Paper, 1s. 6d. ; cloth, 2s. 6d.)

The subtitle, "A Handbook for Singers, Clerical and Lay," indicates its scope. Choirmasters will find it a valuable aid in training their tenors and basses.

The Boy's Voice. J. Spencer Curwen. (Curwen.)

A symposium of great interest, the contributors ranging from cathedral organists to village schoolmasters. As the work is now unfortunately out of print, second-hand copies should be sought.

The Choirboy's Pocket Book. (S.P.C.K. 1s. 6d.)

Practical and comprehensive. There are short biographies of church composers ; historical notes on church music ; twenty pages on "How to Read Music," and Musical Terms and Signs ; notes on behaviour, the Church Calendar, building, vestments, organization, services, the organ, etc. ; prayer ; etc. Nothing could be better for presentation to boys on admission to the choir.

ACCOMPANIMENT

Organ Accompaniment to the Psalms. C. W. Pearce. (Winthrop Rogers. 2s. 6d.)

Both plainsong and Anglican chants are treated. The specimen accompaniments show ingenuity and resource—too much, perhaps, in the case of plainsong. There are interesting chapters on the use of the Psalter.

Varied Harmonies to Hymn-Tunes. Eric Thiman. (Oxford University Press. 2s.)

Short and practical, with chapters on chromatic, diatonic, contrapuntal, imitative, and model harmonies. The numerous music-type examples are good models.

PLAINSONG ACCOMPANIMENT

The Rudiments of Plainsong. Francis Burgess. (*Musical Opinion* Office. 1s.)

The Elements of Plainsong. (Plainsong and Mediæval Music Society. 3s. 6d.)

Accompanying Harmonies for Use with the Manual of Plainsong. W. G. A. Shebbeare. (Novello. 7s.)

Organ Accompaniment to the Ordinary of the Mass. (Plainsong and Mediæval Music Society. 6s.)

Plainsong Accompaniment. J. H. Arnold. (Oxford University Press. 12s. 6d.)

The Teaching and Accompaniment of Plainsong. Francis Burgess. (Novello. 5*s.* 6*d.*)

All these works contain admirable examples of simple modal accompaniment. Mr. Arnold's book deals very thoroughly with the principles.

ORGAN PLAYING

Organ Playing : Its Technique and Expression. A. Eaglefield Hull. (Augener. 4*s.* 6*d.*)

A practical book, rich in music-type examples of typical passages, fully fingered and footed.

Organ Registration. Everett E. Truette. (Boston: Thompson. $2.50.)

A very thorough treatment of the subject. Though written with American instruments in view, its general principles and many of its details apply to English organs.

The Organ and its Music. A. C. Delacour de Brisay. (Kegan Paul. 6*s.*)

A readable account of the history and development of the instrument and its repertory.

GENERAL

Quires and Places Where They Sing. Sydney H. Nicholson. (Bell. 8s. 6d.)

An exhaustive work, containing a history of church music and highly practical chapters on interpretation, choir training, the organist, the place of music in the church service, etc. There is a very full bibliography, and a facsimile of Merbecke's Communion service is given in an Appendix.

Pamphlets of the Church Music Society. (Oxford University Press. 1*d.* to 4*d.* each.)

Music in Worship : Report of the Archbishop's Committee appointed in May, 1922. Revised edition, 1932. (S.P.C.K . 1*s.*)

Contains a comprehensive bibliography.

CONTENTS

PART I

GENERAL SURVEY

PART II

PRACTICAL TEAM WORK

PART III

THE MUSIC: ITS CHOICE AND RENDERING

PART I

GENERAL SURVEY

THERE is something in it of divinity more than the ear discovers : it is an hieroglyphical and shadowed lesson of the whole world, and creatures of God ; such a melody to the ear, as the whole world, well understood, would afford the understanding. In brief, it is a sensible fit of that harmony which intellectually sounds in the ears of God.—SIR THOMAS BROWNE (on Music) : *Religio Medici*.

CHAPTER I

PRELIMINARY DISTINCTIONS

"There is no sound without signification."—St. Paul.

LIKE mathematics, music can well be thought of as both pure and applied. The common chord, for example, is *pure* music. It is everywhere. It is a physical fact in the universe; and can be quietly sounded on any key-board (as nearly in tune as the keyboard can get). It may be used in the home, in the church, the school, the theatre, the open air, in any way, and in any connection whatsoever. And the moment it is so used it virtually becomes *applied* music. Church music may therefore, perhaps, be usefully defined and distinguished from all other music as music applied to the purposes of public worship. This momentarily includes all that the reader may find to be good or bad church music. Ultimately the worshipper decides whether it shall be good or bad; but there are, surely, discernible principles which underlie right choice. There is a music which is inherently fitting for purposes of corporate worship; and it is one of the objects of this book to explore, and, if possible, expound the underlying principles of choice. What makes music "to the good" or not, in church?

We may note at once that not all music at present set to sacred words can be said to fulfil our needs. And to distinguish church music from secular music by classing the first as set to sacred and the second to secular words is impossible.

Think of organ voluntaries, for example. No innately noble strain of music, though first found in connection with secular words, can be banned, provided it sets up no secular associations in the minds of the worshippers. To forbid any such fine strain of music would be to impoverish the voice of Christendom. As well forbid the pulpit utterance of any noble thought that is not of Christian origin. A fine harmonic progression in music is the flower of a fine mind, now and always. Conversely, music inherently frivolous can only be the product of a frivolous condition of mind, whether wedded to sacred words or not.

The reader may naturally doubt his own musical judgment. "How," he asks, "am I to tell a frivolous from a sacred strain, especially if both are set to sacred words?" In a subsequent chapter effort will be made to suggest some of the musical signs of ordinary reverence, aspiration and restraint in church music.

Here it may help to say that average men are probably far better judges of this very matter than they dare to imagine. Picture a newly ordained clergyman who professes no criterion of musical judgment. He loves poetry, and has happened to write a beautiful hymn, let us suppose, for the Dedication Services of his particular church. "How delightful," everyone says,

"to have 'our very own hymn' for this year's service!"
And straightway the organist and a musical parishioner
—say, a churchwarden—both compose a special tune
for the new words (not a wildly unlikely happening).
Now the new vicar is momentarily placed in a dilemma
from which only tact and a sound practical judgment
can free him. We will pretend that the home-made
hymn begins: "O Saviour, dwell in this Thy house";
and that one of the tunes opens as follows:

and the other:

Now let the vicar and his two musical devotees meet
at tea. "How good of you both to have written a tune
for these words! But now we must face the invidious
task of deciding which shall be sung," says the vicar,
cheerfully disguising his anxiety. Next imagine the
churchwarden (who wrote the second tune) breaking in tactfully to make the vicar's task easy by insisting
that the organist has managed to fit these particular
words far better than he. "Mine is tuneful enough,
Vicar," says the churchwarden, "but see how well the
other tune fits the petition." Now comes the point.
Let the reader himself sound these two lines of melody
with the line of the hymn two or three times. Is it

beyond the power of very ordinary men to perceive that the first melody really fits the quiet spirit of the words in a way that the light-hearted disjunct tunefulness of the other does not? The vicar could come, in his turn, to the rescue by saying to the churchwarden: "My dear man—*your* tune, it seems to me, would fit exactly into the children's flower service next month; for, by the way, I have written a small hymn for them also. Look! it fits perfectly! Sing the first line:"

The flowers and all our hearts are gay!

"There!" say all three. And common sense prevails easily.

So far we have only distinguished, first between music pure and applied, then between music to be applied to worship and that applied to other purposes. This leads us a vital step further. For we most of all need today to distinguish quite clearly and with as fine a precision as possible between two great orders of all church music, both capable of being perfected along two markedly different lines. We have to distinguish between (1) all musical utterances used to dispose men to worship, in the way architecture and applied fine art can dispose men to worship; and (2) all musical utterance used as the immediate vehicle of the spirit of worship itself. It may be helpful to set down the distinctions so far made in the form of a genealogical tree:

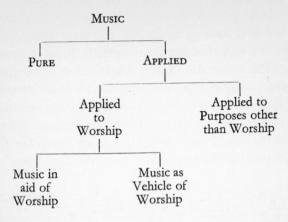

Thus, an Anthem or a Voluntary is definitely music in aid; a Gloria or a Kyrie may be music as the very channel of worship itself. It may perhaps not too tritely be suggested that the aim of an anthem is to be fitly beautiful, and the aim of liturgical music is to be beautifully fitting. Fitness and beauty, like tact and love, are, at root, indistinguishable. Nevertheless, if liturgical music, forsaking its simplicity, tries to be beautiful in itself, it ceases to be fittingly lovely. This fact makes the distinction today seem urgent. For it is clear that, on the one hand, music as elaborate and exactingly complex as the most elaborate architecture in the world can be devotedly offered by church musicians; and it can be as beautifully in place in Westminster Abbey or York Minster as the elaborated architecture itself is in place. On the other hand, it is equally clear that to attempt to make such elaborate music an integral part of the utterance of the musically unskilled worshippers themselves, whether in West-

minster Abbey or anywhere else, is to defeat its true
end. It is like demanding of worshippers that they
should build their own churches and stain their own
glass. We must, for good, open the gates to the two
orders of church music.

The importance of this distinction today lies chiefly
in the double encouragement it will bring to all, when
once understood. Assume that music were, on the one
hand, wanted only as an external aid, disposing men's
minds to thoughts of worship; let its attributes of
melody, harmony, rhythm and design be nobly fitting;
and there remains no perceivable limit to its aspiring
complexity of glories. If, on the other hand, music were
wanted only as a sort of sublimated speech, a public
utterance of public worship, a voice of many made one,
speech made beautiful: then *all* its ideals would lie
definitely in the other direction—completely away from
all the exacting complexities of choral art at its highest;
away from all tonal architecture where the choral
stones are living stones, with wills of their own and
with responsible parts to play in a tonal building, and
exacting the musician's utmost art and practice.

Although the ideals of music in aid of worship do
not exclude the greatest complexity, the ideals of
worship-music are those of primal simplicity. It must
be art still; but, paradoxically, the art of the many at
its best is artless. Beauty it must have, but the beauty
of a simple, spontaneous utterance of natural and
ordinary sense, in sung words, by natural, ordinary
people, whose devotion impels them to speak and
sing as one—"to make one voice to be heard in prais-

ing and thanking the Lord." Congregations must sing as naturally, unaffectedly and unlabouredly as they would speak.

It seems clear from the start that both orders of music here indicated are for ever right. Puritanism may try wholly to banish one ; and what Dr. Frere has called "art-music" (in describing historic plainsong) may try to banish the other. But both undoubtedly have heavenly and neighbourly uses on earth, now ; and they can help and even nourish each other. Confusion of the two, however, and of their aims seems common. Let them be distinct from each other beyond possibility of confusion : the one giving endless outlet for devoted expert service, never, it would seem, excluding a single musical worker who could and would offer to his church his most skilful service ; the other giving an outlet, severely delimited, yet a fine outlet for aspiring musicians, precisely because in its turn it must be music for the "slowest battalion." It must not leave out one single worshipper whose gifts musically may be rudimentary but who joins in the act of worship, whether the words in that act of worship be "said or sung."

It will surely bring instant gain to the Church when once the fundamental distinction between these two orders is made clear by her, recognized by her devotees and avowedly put into practice. One marked result likely to follow would be a gain in actual numbers and calibre in our choirs. Men and women and boys and girls will feel encouraged to work hard at noble music that costs trouble.

It is a natural and common occurrence for quite good choirs to languish because no demand for musical skill and effort is made upon them at their scanty practices—no fine anthem set to learn, no special music to prepare, no expert contribution to work upon, week by week, or evening by evening. Conversely it is equally quite natural and, it must be feared, an equally common occurrence for congregations to feel discouraged because they are called upon to stand wearily, perhaps for a long setting of the Te Deum to music which is neither beautiful enough to hold their attention as hearers, nor simple enough for them to join in—a species of setting which falls lamentably between two stools. In such cases both congregation and choir are "let down"—a condition of things all too common today. It should, forthwith and everywhere, be made impossible. Neither worship nor its music can prosper along such confusing lines.

The position can be clarified by clergy, choirmasters, choirs and congregations. Let leaders, clerical and lay, take congregations and choirs completely into their confidence. Let the needed opportunity be given to dwell upon the two ideals of music in worship in all homely ways, in sermons and at practices, often enough to ensure that when a beautiful anthem, cantata or organ piece is being heard, *all* worshippers should try to dwell with their ears and minds upon the nobly wrought sounds applied to sacred thoughts, exactly as they might dwell with their eyes and minds upon a nobly wrought design in stained glass depicting sacred subjects. And let the ideals of congregational utterance—whether said or sung—be as frankly dwelt upon and clearly expounded from the pulpit and in the practice room. Congregations in many parts of the country still feel it a duty to stand during the anthem, as though they themselves were taking part ; and they sometimes even seem to feel it vaguely desirable to join in. True, their minds must take part, just as they must when the Scriptures are read to them. Whether sacred words are read by the clergy or sung by the choir, the thoughts behind the words are for all. But if people stand up for the sung anthem and join in, they surely should stand and join in with the read lesson. If, however (as seems clear), it is right to sit for the lesson and sermon, it is right to sit for the musical sermon too, though the preacher be a departed composer. Let us away with confusions large and small as quickly as we may, and get down to as fine a two-fold task as ever faced good-willing people.

CHAPTER II

MUSIC IN AID OF WORSHIP

"Bring all heaven before mine eyes."—MILTON.

THIS chapter might well be headed Non-Con-gregational Music, or Non-Liturgical Music. It might even have been given a more repellent title: *Expert Music*, for it deals with music that pre-supposes utmost skill and hard work.

The influence of rare minds can be communicated through words. It can also reach men through eye or ear by visual or aural impression. If it is true that the sight of York Minster or Westminster Abbey or any beautiful church can dispose ordinary men's minds to worship as they sit in the nave and look around, and surrender themselves to all the signs of beauty that surround them, no less surely the sound of the Halle-lujah Chorus or the "St. Anne" fugue or any beautiful anthem can do the very same thing, perhaps even more movingly. If it is true that an east window, full of light and depicting suggestions of the story of Christen-dom, can help men, women and children to concen-trate upon the story and realize it more vividly, so can Bach's Passion Music or Elgar's "Apostles." The worshipper has no personal part to play in the beautiful thing seen or heard, except to receive, see or hear in reverence what is offered in reverent aid.

There is danger in the widespread failure to think

of music *as a reality*. A church melody is as real a thing as a chancel or a pulpit, and may be as real an influence for good or evil and as really a thing to be treasured, improved or banished. It seems hard to attain this, because, unlike a chancel or a pulpit, an anthem is evanescent, invisible, intangible. It is over and gone in a few moments, whereas a building stays there for anyone to go again on Monday morning and look at for himself. Let it be realized that sounds made to be heard in churches today are as real and as surely *things*, to be as fitly provided and reverently used as are the buildings themselves; and, further, let incumbents and church authorities but realize that they are *as responsible for the one as for the other*, and rapid improvement in church music is certain to follow.

Unfortunately, cultured men of authority today often modestly elude responsibility in the mistaken belief that music is outside their comprehension. Musical connotations—all the associated meanings accumulated through usage in a chord as in a word—may indeed be beyond them, but the man who claims to have no ear for musical meanings will yet readily admit the ability to detect the trend of a speaker's mind by the mere tones of his utterance. In the same way as Greek may remain "Greek" to him, Music may remain "music"; yet in both he may detect character in trend and behaviour despite his ignorance of the language.

The classification of church music with church architecture, church windows, and with all other church art brings two immediate advantages. Church music of this type is seen at once for what it really is in two ways. It is seen to be a matter for the exercise of unlimited care and skill and, if need be, unlimited complexity of detail, demanding from musicians the utmost and most devoted labour and effort to perfection of which they are capable. And, secondly, it is seen, with all other church art, to be animated by but a single motive, that of joyous devotion to what may be called the Beauty of Wholeness.

An urgent question may occur to the reader at this point: How can an act of such complex corporate skill, involving many gifts and performers, be kept devotional? Let us attempt a reply.

Complexity of deed and simplicity of motive are in no way incompatible. They are permanently complementary. All art is a manifold deed of the mind, whether wrought in stones or tones, wood, metal, needlework, pigment, stained glass, or any other medium whatsoever. And in music, pre-eminently, this joyous deed of the mind may have infinite wealth of detail and a single unifying aim. There may be a million strands of thought with a single motive. Indeed, the more complex the detail, the more imperative the need and incentive for the single motive. So it becomes clear that, while ambition to attempt music that is too difficult or complex for their powers is quite a common and uncomfortable failing among well-meaning musical churchmen, yet no limit must be set (except the limits of tact and fitness) upon church music of this order undertaken in the right spirit. *The cure for this ill lies in more work rather than in more modesty.*

Music has a way of attaining complexity without confusion when it becomes animated by strong enough exuberance. Think of such anthems as Weelkes's "Hosanna," Purcell's "O sing unto the Lord," Wesley's "Praise the Lord," Mendelssohn's "Why rage fiercely the heathen," or Harris's "Fair is the heaven," and it will be realized how, when the composer is animated with a single pressing aim, that of giving the ecstasy of the words their fit musical counterpart, his musical technique becomes simple in aim and in its demands upon the hearer, though it may be far from simple in its demands upon choral skill. Lavish practice is needed for any one of these works—practice which is itself devotion, after its own kind, bringing its own reward in the power to go on to more and more beautiful things.

Choirs who thus work hard for their church deserve concurrent acknowledgment of their field of work; and they may often stand in need of the assurance that their work is both needed and welcomed. Congregations and clergy need to realize that the compact is never complete until the music which the choir devotedly try to make, the listeners will in their turn as devotedly receive and responsively contemplate.

It seems well to try here to consider the nature of the whole order of voluntary music in worship, and the main principles that govern it. How can we ensure fitness in anthem, cantata, organ voluntary or sacred symphony? How can we be sure what kind of music the Church should endeavour to encourage and attain?

The possible replies are so manifold that it is hard to choose and regulate those upon which we most need to dwell. Broadly speaking, it is easy to hear (at an aural glance) certain orders of music which do fit church worship and others which do not. Stately choral harmonies, for example, with grace of movement and a reticent yet glowing tone, seem inherently right. Scrappy rhythms many times reiterated, or ungraceful angular melody, or sensational changes of power, all appear to be just as inherently unfit for worshipful purposes.

But on what principles are we to search for standards of fitness? We know that there is often acute difference between quite devout and single-minded churchmen on this very point, where personal taste counts; and underneath these differences there must lie reasons. Careful search for these will tend to clarify, and in God's goodness unify, churchly taste. We humans must count our musical lot to be just the ordinary erring human lot of a changing vision and disciplined journey—a vision of ever more perfect music and an untiring journey towards it. Such a vision of inspiring church music (to be at last as perfect in its kind as the architecture of our Cathedrals already is in its kind) was never more needed by churchmen than today. Classical music itself progressed by leaps and bounds. Earnest men continue to emulate it and adequately perform it. But church music has for long been deplorably confused and inadequately rendered. Let us try to catch at least a glimpse of the possible future. We may propose for

this purpose four criteria of judgment—Originality,
Simplicity, Temper, and Sensitivity.

(1) First, the age-long battle of tastes as between old
and new may be considered, for it works disastrously
and tries to fix unfortunate limitations to the work of
church musicians: limitations with which all must be
familiar, and which are natural enough and not necessarily wilful. The reader may often have heard a bad
anthem praised, for no other reason than that the
congregation have liked it since they were children;
and a really fine piece of music resented by those who
have "never heard it before." On the other hand,
he may hear folk exclaim that they are "sick of the
same old Easter anthem year after year"; or "thank
Heaven, we have heard a novelty in our church at
last!" Behind these common inclinations, two for
and two against both kinds of music (whether good
or bad in itself), there may be detected the hand
of a Providence which has ordained that all men shall
both long after and pursue in their time *both the
old and the new*. It is good to be able to say "yes"
to both. If we were not musical conservatives at
heart we should lose our way and for ever have to
begin again; and if we were not musical radicals at
heart also we should lapse into deadly idolatry of
"tradition," and find ourselves settling down and
actually saying "no" to good music. The best in-
novators are the humblest reverers of tradition; while
the best conservers of the past are those to whom the
common chord is still so new and heavenly a thing that
nothing could be newer or more worthy of devoted

labour than to use it and sing it as glowingly as our fathers sang it. The man who exclaims against the new anthem is temporarily detained by prejudice. He is momentarily disqualified for the new because the old has not yet been completed *for him*. How we all, as conservatives, can and do long to hear, for example, "If ye love me" by Tallis once perfectly rendered today! And how new it would sound! Conversely, the man who exclaims against the old is temporarily incapable of understanding it, because rebellious against the apparent inertia of those who are not yet ready to move on.

Safety and a sound judgment seem to lie in fearless recognition and love of both orders, as though they were at one. Such recognition does not perhaps make at once for ease. But there is a chastened contentment in the thought that our pains can be growing pains. Ideally, delights in the new and old are twin delights. To pit them against each other in the matter of church music as if they were two divided ideals is to have no notion of their complementary nature and true use. Still worse is it to divide individual men who are fellow-workers into champions of the old order on the one side and of the new on the other. Partiality of outlook and political methods of controversy are obviously fatal in church music, whatever they may be elsewhere.

So a fearless and faithful "Yes" alike both to the old and the new is our first advice in this matter of musical discrimination. The best upholder of tradition among us is the best reformer. He sings the old music as though the ink were barely dry upon the copy. He sings it as a heavenly novelty that exactly fits the needs of congregations today, and if it does not fit them he abandons it. He also sings the new anthem as though it had for ever been ; to him it has merely lain undiscovered till today. In such a temper of mind, curiously enough, church musicians are happily equipped to choose a future corpus of church music. For, by tastes which may seem superficially contradictory, we all find ourselves thrown back and forth upon first principles. We are thrown back to an old which is new because it rings true today. We are thrown forward to seek the brave and new, which would have rung just as true ages ago had it been due to be discovered then. The one word *original*, in its two accepted senses, curiously sums up the quality which distinguishes the two-fold Christian treasure described by our Lord as "things new and old." We need in church, even more than anywhere else, this highest of all qualities called originality.

We may venture, then, to formulate the gist of these thoughts as a first working principle of choice, thus :

Music in aid of worship must be original in the two distinct senses of being something quite new and something so old that it has been there from the beginning.

(2) SIMPLICITY: Is not the comprehensive quality just described always the hall-mark of that which men call inspiration ? And, surprisingly enough, it may be seen that even the simplest common chord can be put to most original use today and tomorrow. "What!" the modern reader may well exclaim, "has church music got no further than that ? Can the commonest common-

place of musical phraseology, already used for centuries, be suggested as a basis for new and inspired music tomorrow or a hundred years hence?" Yes; highest value for simplest things seems the next serviceable criterion of musical choice.

Chaucer's poem on the daisy tells how he went on his knees and gazed upon one square inch of God's earth with rapture, to watch the "day's eye" open. Those who can so value an inch of a field can best possess the whole field. This seems to be the meaning of the Beatitude of the meek who "inherit the earth." Any church composer who can love a common chord with the fervour of a Chaucer will naturally inherit the whole field of music today and tomorrow. Highest evaluation of the simplest things will always tend to renew church music. Its present lamentable shortcomings are largely traceable to the cheap holding of common chords, so cheap that the most slovenly presentment of them is tolerated widely and continuously. And such slovenliness itself obscures the very nature of church music, and thwarts development. Christian music seems at its strongest when Christian fervour pours itself lavishly into common chords. It was in common chords that Palestrina saved music for the Church in the sixteenth century. And it is significant that a work such as Vaughan Williams's Mass in G minor, built from beginning to end of nothing but common chords, can sound quite splendidly new. This is not to extol the common chord as an end, but rather as a perpetual and benignant beginning of good things.

This second working principle of choice may perhaps be formulated thus:

Music in aid of worship must set high evaluation on simple forms of Beauty, such as common chords and restrained diatonic melody.

(3) TEMPER: But chords are only euphonies; they are like well-blended colours. We need a principle of choice that may at least tend to show us how these euphonies and colours should be used in church. Originality and simplicity are not enough. Fitness is crucial. Let a curate move to the lectern, for example, with the simple joy in mere movement that Chaucer found in kneeling before the daisy, and he might dance like a child to read the lesson—and shock the whole church! Fitness of movement, of deportment, is obviously a subject so important to all in practice, and in all departments, that we must try to formulate a basic principle of action (that is, of *rhythm*) in church, which may be useful.

It is perhaps true that our two first principles cannot but lead to fitting behaviour or movement in every musical contingency. And our third principle will in reality be of the nature of a rider to the other two. Sincerity and high values in music are likely to lead to fitting musical behaviour. And Behaviour is Rhythm. Of all anthems and voluntaries, it seems true to say, "By their rhythms ye shall know them." It may quite safely be laid down that violent or protuberant contrasts are unfitting in church music. Rhythms with short trivial patterns often repeated (as it were for their own sake) are not likely to occur, if only for the simple reason that

3

any feature in music which is sensational, or small-minded, or oft-repeated, calls attention to itself and defeats its own end in doing so. Repetition is in all music and is vital, but rarely or never for its own sake. Strong contrasts can also be in place in church, wherever they fitly subserve a wonderful end (as do Wesley's startling chords in "Blessed be the God and Father"). Even a small-minded scrap of childish rhythm could be in place in church where, again, it serves some lovely end—as, for example, in a cradle song of the Infant Jesus, sung perhaps as part of a Nativity cantata. But, generally speaking, it seems too clear to need exposition that all church music will favour long-minded and large-minded rhythm, full of life yet equable, free from sensational changes or any ostentatious display of skill. In choral music the rhythms will be subservient at every point in every way to the motive and inspiration of the words set; in instrumental, the rhythmic thrust will be equally subject to the motive of worship in the service of which it is part. There are, for example, choral preludes for the organ on tunes of sacred association which make perfect voluntaries for contemplative and quiet services; and there are glorious fugues and sonatas for organ and other instruments which ideally embody the spirit of constancy, perseverance, joy, indomitable effort, and love of perfect form, of harmony and of the beauty of wholeness. These played with mastery can make a fitting "second sermon." There are, on the other hand, voluntaries which leave a mere impression of gaiety, display and even sensationalism. Such can receive no inner sanction for church uses, and are to be ruled out.

On the choral side there are oratorios, cantatas and anthems which use music's fullest resources to carry the story of Christ's life, death, resurrection and ascension vividly to the heart and mind. Even these will be subject to the two simple principles already named, and to the further rule of rhythmic fitness which may be set down in some such form as this :

Music in aid of worship needs to be rhythmically strong, but not rhythmically assertive. In church music, the rhythm will subserve the motive of the words set. In instrumental music it will tend to combine strong enthusiasm with restraint in long equable phrases.

(4) SENSITIVITY: It is likely that many minds will associate the fulfilment of this ruling with the astonishingly gentle strength of Bach in his finest church music. With the technique of a giant and the heart of a child, his devout mind and simple love of his Lord transmuted and blended his thoughts about the Cross, about death and future heavenly joys, into a kind of church music that points a marvellous way to all comers who can discern it.

But it is not only the composer who needs to attain the felicities of sensitivity. It is not only the Bachs and Chaucers who need joyous original impulse and high evaluation of common things. Some practical ruling must yet be added for the guidance of the musical team. Choirs and players who have to interpret apt music need to attain team-aptness too. A choral ensemble happens to afford one of the most

perfect examples on earth of the ordinary social virtue
of an alert and habitual give-and-take. The mere ex-
penditure of team-effort needed for the perfecting of
one choral common chord, held quietly but purposefully, in good tune, not merely mobilizes the exacting
qualities of discipline and self-effacement to an almost
unique degree; it also raises the value of a single chord
to a measureless and ever-increasing extent. (This must
sound extravagant to all but those who have tried to
induce team-sensitization even in highly trained choirs.)
With practical choral difficulties and demands in mind,
it may be helpful to summarize this fourth team-
requirement as follows :

*Music in aid of worship needs collective sensitization to
timing, toning and tuning, raised to their highest powers in
all choral and instrumental ensemble.*

At the moment of trying to word such a ruling, one
is painfully aware that it is a mere counsel of perfection. Leaders of many good-willing amateur choral
bodies today will breathe a sad *non possumus* as they
read. But let such readers reflect for a moment upon
the discipline normally required of secular teams who
perform for profit or display, or for purchased amuse-
ment of others in public places. Do choirmasters
demand enough of themselves and of their choirs ?
The first requirement is not technical perfection, but
the steady will towards perfection. (Not that the choral
will can for ever be taken for the choral deed !) This
being realized, it is enough that a church choir should
journey steadily towards its choral perfection. The
journey's the thing here and now, not the goal. And it

should be remembered that the fact that church music of any complexity involves unity *in excelsis* to bring it to a real hearing is greatly in its favour, since it means the mobilization of a working and unfailing neighbourliness, the very thing for which Christianity itself stands.

We have now perhaps reached a point from which we may try to sum up the essential nature of all voluntary music in aid of Christian worship. It will be a music that proves simple to listeners, hard to performers. It will have primal beauty and attractiveness for the ears and minds of all men. It will never be individualistic or idiosyncratic, but will speak, in unmistakably human tones, from first to last. To sit for a moment at St. Paul's feet, the church musician does not speak "in tongues," just for his own "building up." He utters or uses twelve notes (or less) "with understanding" rather than "ten thousand in a tongue." This does not mean that he may not put his five or seven or twelve notes to ten thousand different uses. Nor does it mean that unlearned men cannot receive music of ten thousand notes which only learned men can write. That would be like saying that none but architects can worship in a Cathedral, or, to descend to more perishable appetites, none but *chefs* could enjoy a banquet.

All this leads to a useful thought that is perhaps too often forgotten by church-music enthusiasts. Is it pertinent to offer in public worship that which does not meet the real necessity of those present? Do they feel any urgent need for Beauty? From the King himself down to his humblest subject, from the

Archbishop down to the humblest parishioner of the humblest village, we know that we could safely offer, for example, clear water to allay their common thirst, or a piece of bread to allay a common hunger, and the congenial atmosphere of human comfort to allay a common sorrow. If it be indeed true that there is *nothing* in music (or in Beauty generally) that meets just such a common need of men, then we must not be deluded; for in such a case music would be a permanent impertinence in public worship, whatever it may be elsewhere. We must go further and admit that even if music when perfectly offered should meet a primal need, even if Beauty seen or heard can be a profound aid to all true worshippers, it may still easily be that perfect music *imperfectly* sounded is worse than irrelevant and disturbing. Furthermore, even if music and its rendering should *both be perfectly fitting*, there is still a contingency that worshippers themselves may fail us. They may either receive music pertinently and to their gain, or impertinently to their loss, should they be by unfortunate upbringing and associations so perversely disposed as only to hear in music a display of skill by musicians; or only a mild sedative; or an equally mild form of sensational stimulus.

Fortunately all the handicaps just indicated, though actual and even prevalent today, are such as may be dispelled.

The vital question that here faces us concerns the nature of Devotion itself. To reduce it to its simplest terms, two questions may be proposed: Is the communication of perfect and purposeful and intelligible har-

mony from mind to mind by any means—whether
through lines of architecture seen or tones of music
heard—inherently capable of aiding men to worship? If the answer is "Yes," then how can we be
sure of choosing from among all music the right
music?

In reply to the first question, the writers can only
state their belief, constantly confirmed by experience,
that there are certain beautiful orders of rhythm, of
melody and of harmony which seem utterly to fit the
mind set upon Christian worship. It may even be that
the exactly fitting music can *induce* the mind to worship. But exact fitness, as we all know, is a very large
order in public worship. It implies knowledge of the
congregation's musical sensitiveness to, and existing associations with, current orders of rhythm, melody and
harmony—current musical idiom—as well as profound
knowledge of the inherent qualities of these three main
factors in music.

In answer to the supplementary question we may
turn for a moment to actual evidences which go to show
how strongly and deeply an ordinary gathering of men
and women can be touched by pure music. Three small
personal experiences which have tended, among numberless like experiences, to confirm this belief in the
writer's own mind may be relevant to the reader's
thoughts at this point. The first happened at a lecture
to a crowded audience of working men, with women
and children (and even babies), in Wales. The lecture
hall was crowded and stuffy. A very poor piano was at
hand, and on it, in illustration of some point in the

lecture, a perfect fourth was played *pianissimo*. The silence of attention became suddenly intense, prolonged and unforgettable. The second experience was in Yorkshire, where at a Festival some small talk on choral technique was going forward. A chord of C was played, and the audience was asked, quite unwarned, to try a choral experiment by singing the words "rest in peace" upon this one chord. This again, creating a mysteriously beautiful choral rhythm, was uncannily impressive. It gave an opportunity for that magical effect which is always produced by a mass of people doing the exact opposite of what is so often called "singing *out*." Everybody was probably "singing *in*." As Fénelon somewhere says, they were unconsciously "taking counsel with their Beloved"; and the same primal wonderment was observable as in Wales in the case of the perfect fourth. The third instance of this kind of unearthly deep listening was at a concert given in a prison, where, as all may guess, a sentimental song or a comic story would be expected to bring the most natural response and relief. A violinist, however, chose to play Gluck's melody of the Elysian fields from "Orfeo." Certainly it was played with great beauty, reticence and simplicity. Here again, not only was the silence of listening palpable and profound from all the convicts and everyone else, but the *quality* of the enjoyment seemed neither that which is associated with the thing we call sentiment, nor the thing we call entertainment. It seemed a state of enjoyment and wonderment, akin to mental illumination.

It is not suggested that these slender experiences

prove anything. They merely lead one the more keenly to look for the style and the kind of melody, rhythm and harmony which may bring about like results in all churches at the time of worship. Since apparently such thrilling experiences can come with little or no effort except the effort of loving fitness and efficient workmanship, it is hard to imagine that the secret is remote.

Let us, then, venture for the moment to assume that the need is universal; that the hunger of man for the elemental experience of harmony in music (or in any kindred utterance of beauty that is offered) is clear and as natural as other hunger. It has its limitations, but it is there. No "specialist" music will do for this high purpose. No fairy dishes will fit this elemental hunger. The diet must be simply relevant. The thing offered must be offered in forms both intelligible and acceptable. Neither unintelligible musical subtleties (however welcome to the learned) nor intelligible cacophony (however welcome to the sensationalist) will meet the case in church. Even with these inhibitions or negative warnings, the positive means are still limitless. As we have seen, there is music in simplest rhythms and melodies and chords of completely intelligible beauty to the plain man, of which endless new uses remain to be revealed. A scholarly clergyman and musician remarked not long ago that he supposed all the possible good Anglican chants "had been written already." He would be astonished, on looking carefully, to find how few chants have so far used such primal melodic inflections as the following:

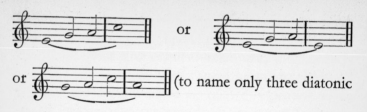

or (to name only three diatonic

phrases) which could have been enjoyable and inspiring to all men any time these thousand years! Now, is it inconceivable that a thousand years hence, if such phrases were sung with the reverent skill and quietude bestowed upon Gluck's F major melody as played to convicts, any little choir anywhere could fail to bring the same intense "hear-a-pin-drop" silence, and the same wondering, worshipful spirit to any congregation of men and women? It is not too much to say that the very endlessness of simply beautiful form in music tells us all clearly that church music has really only just begun.

To conclude, the music offered in aid of Christian worship must be original, setting the highest value on the simplest musical factors (such as conjunct diatonic melody and common chords), magnanimous in its rhythms, with a tireless team-mind bent on reverent efficiency in *ensemble*. There will be irrepressible life in such music, pushing its way into everything sung or played, just as sap pursues a resistless way into a tree's every branch and twig. Nature's vital way is also music's way. But some homely qualifying rules will be needed for the church musician's practical guidance: Let all sorrowful music have a ring of health; in all exuberant music remember the Cross. To every choral *fortissimo* give the refinement of a *pianissimo*; and let every *pianissimo* hold within it the vitality of a *fortissimo*—incipient, not repressed. Real music deals with realities. No easy make-believes will serve in church. "Sweetly pretty anthems" may enervate the Christian as he journeys. Sweetness there will be, but strength with it. Church art is of necessity wholesome. It sets out not only to aid worship fittingly at every point, but to make the artist's "beauty of wholeness," referred to earlier, approach the Beauty of Holiness itself.

CHAPTER III

MUSIC AS A MEANS OF WORSHIP

"Jesus saith unto them, 'Fill the water-pots with water.' And they filled them up to the brim. And he saith unto them, 'Draw out now, and bear unto the Governor of the feast.'"—JOHN ii. 7, 8.

IF song were not at least as natural and spontaneous a human act as speech, there would be no question of music becoming an actual carrier of public worship itself. It could still be an aid, perhaps, as described in the previous chapter. But men could never have sung the very words of their worship together.

There seems to have existed a common notion that art as a whole is something opposed to nature. "Thus to walk is natural, to dance is an art," says Johnson's Dictionary. This enormously narrows the meaning of the words *art* and *nature*. Both seem to lose their inner meaning in the process. A child who is too happy to walk and begins to dance does not suddenly become unnatural. What old Johnson would say is that the moment it began to dance according to custom, the moment it began to keep the "rules of the game," it would cross the border from nature to art—from nature that is in too high spirits to walk, to art that uses those high spirits to organize a dance. But seek how one may to agree with Johnson's distinction, or to distil helpful meaning out of it, one is bound to set it aside as something very much less than the truth about speaking and singing in church. The words set at the head of the chapter seem to come nearer the true relation of the act of speech with the art of song.

Fill the carrying vessels of speech (that is, the words) with their full meaning. Pour spirit into their every cranny and crevice, their every vowel, aspirate, and consonantal edge "to the brim," and the musical miracle is sure to happen. In some real sense, the ordinary well-springs of human utterance in words are turned into "wine"—that is, into song. The most striking direct illustration of this at the present time is perhaps to be found in the Welsh (so-called) *hwyl* of impassioned speakers. *Hwyl* means Sail. When a preacher is "in full sail" in Wales, it is not forbidden, or out of the way, or disturbing to the congregation if his delivery becomes completely musical, and he begins to *chant* his thoughts. Dr. Lloyd Williams has made a careful study of contemporary *hwyl*; and he has described it as rising from time to time, at important moments, by a perfect fourth; then inflecting again at the new level. He has also noticed that the *hwyl* ultimately tends to fall into the Dorian Mode, and the present writer has heard a preacher in Llandovery break into the following clearly marked, impulsive and beautiful chant or melodic phrase while preaching :

which entirely bore out the Dorian theory.

But one formidable, perpetual problem faces us in regard to enthusiastic speech turning into song or chant. A single child may dance for joy naturally, as Johnson knew well enough. A preacher may rise into fervent chant equally naturally. But there must be rules of agreement when many dance together by consent; and congregations cannot rise into song without a regulation or two. How is unanimity to become unisonority? How can spontaneity be organized, and yet remain spontaneous? It must be both: for if it is not, how can the miracle happen? If the plainest of plain song (using the word in its all-embracing sense) is to be used at a given moment in the public worship of, say, any hundred men and women of goodwill, with natural manners and an elementary knowledge of melody, then it must plainly be prearranged. And is there such a thing in heaven or earth as a prearranged miracle?

Here lies our most engrossing natural problem in this simplest order of church music. Approached from the side of natural speech, when a congregation inspired to worship utters the words, "O Lord, make haste to help us," or responds to the glorious salutation, "Lift up your hearts," with the words, "We lift them up unto the Lord," they must be care-free; and their speech-inflection, their speech-rhythm, and the light and shade of their utterance, must all be such as naturally and spontaneously carry the spirit and sense of the utterance.

When a congregation is minded to turn such words into melody, they must be enabled to fit their natural melodic inflection, melodic rhythm, and light and shade to a definite tune in due deference to one another. Then further, if there is vocal harmony even of the simplest kind, the problem is intensified fourfold. It must all be care-free yet care-full; unstudied yet studiously fitted, voice with voice; spontaneously uttered words *plus* carefully co-ordinated song. And neither of the two at any point must belie each other.

The recent spate of speech-rhythm psalters testifies to the timely and even intense interest in this important question among church choirs and congregations. Speech-rhythms and music-rhythms are in search of each other, looking for their most reasonable unity in good chanting. But speech-rhythm presents only one side of the question; and we must try here to get as comprehensive a view as possible of the whole problem. Before doing so, it is well to remind ourselves that the present ignorance among cultured men and women of the bare elements of melody ought not to be allowed to remain the barrier it has too long been. The opportunities for hearing music through broadcasting will gradually increase general discernment; and when intelligent and efficient choral song is made the normal thing in every school, and never left to chance, common-sense will see to it that infants in every nursery and infant-school are made as familiar with the sight of a musical stave of five lines:

and with a common chord set on its lines:

or in its spaces: as they are

with the C, A, T, of cat, or D, O, G, of dog, and at just as early an age. For the one is quite as easy as the other. It is strange that their clear order of importance is generally reversed. The result is a musically uneducated nation. We may usefully wonder how many of the six hundred and fifteen Members of Parliament, how many public men, leading scientists, headmasters, bishops, priests or deacons—to say nothing of how many ordinary men and women in any educated congregation—would count it as much an impossibility to read and sing the first at sight (quite a babyish task really) as it would be an impossible insult to be asked to spell and speak the second! Such an abnormal defect in the education of civilized man will naturally in time be removed, probably through the aid of broadcasting.

Looking, then, with reasoned confidence towards the day when every normal man and woman in an ordinary Christian congregation will be able to read a chant or a scrap of melody on its stave as easily as they read the words of a hymn, it will be well to look into the nature of the alliance between words and melody. It is obvious at a glance that the recent attention to speech-rhythms is but a beginning, and at present a one-sided beginning, touching but one dimension of the alliance. The constant contradictions that have arisen between beautiful prose in the psalms and beautiful melody in chants become flagrant when the chant insists on being in itself a metrical affair. The style of chant which slowly evolved, and is now known as Anglican, can, at its best, be marvellously expressive and fitting. At its worst, it becomes an arrogant and self-satisfied short-metre hymn-tune. Now, the metrical versified psalms may fit a metrical diversified little part-song. Thus, while this kind of chanting of unmetrical lines can be an abuse and a misfit when sung metrically :

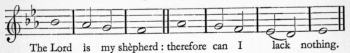

The Lord is my shèpherd : therefore can I   lack nothing.

the Scottish paraphrase of the same verse would fit the Anglican "short-metre tune" :

The Lord my shep-herd is,   And want I   nev - er shall.

We may examine the fundamental position a little more closely by putting to ourselves three questions :

(1) What are the chief *elements of utterance* which naturally come into play in speech the moment a man utters his mind aloud ?

(2) How are those elements affected when many speak together aloud by consent ?

(3) Are the chief *elements of melodic utterance* sufficiently like those of speech for the two to run quite naturally in double harness ?

(1) In speech the most vital elements of utterance seem to be five :

(*a*) Rise and fall, or relative *Pitch* of words ;
(*b*) Rhythm, or relative *Length* of words ;
(*c*) Light and shade, or relative *Volume* ;
(*d*) *Speed* ;
(*e*) *Spacing*.

Before considering these briefly in turn, it should be noted that there is a sixth factor of great importance,

4

which seems best omitted here (though it may be considered tentatively at a later stage)—the factor of actual *quality* of voice. As this is largely an involuntary factor in every speaker, and one that is also physically inherited, it seems better to leave it out. It is true that much may be done by individual attention, at least now and again, to the golden rule of *listening to one's own noises as one utters them* and then choosing and cultivating the least unpleasant qualities of tone in the voice, which is our life-companion "for better, for worse"; yet it seems better not to try too closely to enter into so personally conditioned an element. Quality resembles *shape* or *calibre*. We speak of a round quality, or a piercing quality of voice. "My name means the *shape* I am," proudly exclaimed Humpty-Dumpty to Alice. And a man's reading voice is rather like the "shape he is" mentally; gainly or ungainly, all church speakers and church singers alike had best try to reach a point where they can mutually forget both their own and each others' actual shape or quality of voice.

We may now dwell analytically on each of the five elements of utterance named above :

(*a*) PITCH.—The rise and fall in pitch (or vibration-frequency) of the speaking voice we will call *speech-inflection*. Here is an approximate graph of an actual voice, while speaking a specimen verse of the Venite :

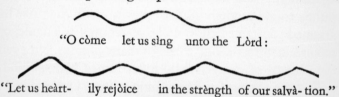

"O còme   let us sìng   unto the Lòrd :

"Let us heàrt-   ily rejòice   in the strèngth of our salvà- tion."

The reader may for himself, or with the help of a quick-eared friend, discover varieties of natural speech-inflection in speaking and reading. These become very interesting as registers of actual shades of thought, and ultimately of character as well. Natural diffidence or inertia registers monotonously, for example, in the conversational voice of many a parson, and it drops inaudibly low at final syllables ; while a neighbourly desire that chief syllables shall, at all costs, be heard in every corner of the church will cause the same voice to rise serviceably and save the situation. In taking "graphs" of speech-inflections, it is well to trace the rise and fall of each phrase, *i.e.*, of each sentence or part of a sentence uttered in a single length, in one breath and with no audible break. This should be done in a series of single lines written down in a sequence resembling blank verse. When done systematically, it will be seen that phrase-graphs tend towards a definite melodic shape. Individual tendencies will emerge as well as general tendencies. Broadly speaking, there seems a general inclination to move to a highest vocal point at a chief syllable in each phrase or unit. This rise and fall quite unconsciously registers rise and fall of mental energy or urgency. A voice pressing a point in argument will tend to rise (on the pointed syllables) time and again higher and higher, like a schoolboy trying in high-jumps to get a notch higher every time till the prize be attained. Sustained effort will register itself in a tendency to sustained monotone through many phrases, but even then scraps of characteristic inflection of various kinds will occur at closes and breathing points. Canon Ainger (who was a wonderful reader) used to tell of some friendly counsel, which he himself had received, to raise his voice at the end of each sentence. He did so habitually, and his hearers never ceased to bless him for it. There is a story of a City man who declared himself cured of ill-temper by a vow never to allow his voice to rise above a certain pitch—to the lasting advantage of his associates. A generous, highly imaginative mind will tend to speak over a very wide compass. It is said that Canon Dalton's voice would cover two octaves in reading the lessons. He himself used humbly to remark that his voice "went like that." But he did not mind what people thought or said. His self-regard was as slender as his regard for vocal propriety, and both were in inverse ratio to his reverence for, and vital interest in, the Spirit as revealed in the lesson itself.

(*b*) LENGTH.—The longs and shorts of speech in English are astonishingly communicative. It is possible to conceive of languages in which they signify little. But the artificial lengthening of a single syllable can distort an English utterance beyond repair ; and, conversely, the failure to dwell upon what may be called the *carrying* syllables can severely handicap the spirit and sense of any utterance. For example, let the reader quietly and naturally utter these words half a dozen or more times, in ways that seem best to carry their meaning :

> "And God said, let there be light :
> And there was light";

or these :

> "Let us heartily rejoice in the strength of our salvation."

After saying such sentences many times over, and listening closely, he will find that certain syllables will naturally have grouped themselves as *shorts*, leading up to a long syllable, and in this way definite speech-rhythms will gradually emerge. These rhythms are never inflexible; but they are always indispensable. Equalize the lengths of all syllables for a single sensible sentence, and in English the result sounds nothing short of imbecile. Or try lengthening any syllable which by nature is not long in the course of a sentence—such as the word "God" in the first example :

"And *God* said, let there be light ;"

and, with the best intentions, the result will sound unnatural and affected. Or try shortening a naturally long syllable such as the word "true" in :

"That was the true light ;"

and another kind of serious distortion arises. On the other hand, let the long vowel in "heartily," the diphthong and sibilant in "rejoice," the deep *ng* sound in "strength," and the long *a* in "salvation" all have their careful dues, and the vigour and variety of natural speech-rhythm will become apparent in such common and oft-repeated phrases of worship as in, "Let us heartily rejoice in the strength of our salvation."*

* The following are musically-noted speech-rhythms taken from life :

And God said, let there be light: and there was light.

Let us hear-ti-ly re-joice in the strength of our sal-va-tion.

I went by, and lo, he was gone: I sought him, but his

place could no-where be found.

(*c*) VOLUME.—In all verbal utterance, the element of tonal strength, or volume, counts perhaps for more than any other element in the general physical and unconscious effect upon the hearer. The speaker also is unconsciously affected by the way his voice "lets off steam." Thus a man has only suddenly to double the loudness of his speech to give the impression of doubling the urgency with which he feels and communicates it. Softening of the voice has just as significant an effect the other way. A steady increase of volume will indicate a steady rise of interest and keenness in the speaker ; and the decline of urgency is as surely signified by a *diminuendo* in the speaking. Here, again, the reader will find an experiment or two useful. Read the first line of Gray's Elegy in a stentorian voice :

ff "The curfew tolls the knell of parting day."

Now read this line from Browning in a very soft tone :

pp "O, the wild joys of living ! the leaping from rock to rock."

Or try the effect of a gradual loudening, a gradual softening, and then of a sudden change of volume at any given point. The element of loudness in speech may be well compared to the dimension of thickness or bulk in any material object. No delicate thought will bear shouting, nor can three cheers be easily given in a whisper.

(*d*) SPEED.—Apart altogether from the relative speeds of short and long syllables in speech, the general speed in delivery is a permanent and telling element of utterance. It can make or mar the effect upon the hearer. Thus, all other things being equal, rapid delivery of momentous words has a casual, cursory, irreverent effect; conversely, very slow, deliberate delivery of unimportant words is dull and deadening. Both are impertinent. The right quickening of speech at the fitting moment can have an electric effect upon the hearer. This element seems peculiarly subject to the general law of *fitness*; or, to give it its ethical and possibly priggish name, *neighbourliness*. It simply is not the game for anyone, be he layman or priest, schoolboy or bishop, to rattle through the most profound prayers at a speed with which the most reverent and intelligent congregation could not possibly keep pace in their minds.

At this point it is perhaps well to note that *speed* in speech is normally a sign of *energy* behind it, from whatever source that energy may come, or to whatever aim it may be directed. In this, natural speed and natural pitch of voice go inseparably together in effect. Nothing could perhaps illustrate this point more convincingly than an experiment with a gramophone record of speech. Set the speeds at (*a*) normal, (*b*) extremely rapid, (*c*) extremely slow. Normal speech is utterly distorted: at one extreme it sounds hysterical and flippant, at the other pompous and lethargic. But the impressive thing about the experiment is that at the extremes the character of the speaker seems wholly changed, in two opposite ways, and in both cases to the bad; both are worse than a mere caricature of normal features. Both suggest a fundamental loss of common sensibility—one may almost say of common decency. This experiment will well repay every student of speech or song.

(e) SPACING.—Sir Walter Parratt used to say to his pupils : "Don't forget to play your *rests*." It is not easy to exaggerate the importance of spacing words in speech. The silences between words are an integral, and even dynamic part of their utterance. Spacing is therefore a fifth and positive element in speech. As well leave out all spaces between words on a written page as leave out the silences, or relative silences, between them in speaking. The extra edges of silence round an important word are as helpful as the extra white mount can be round an etching. For example, a preacher in giving out a significant text, such as "God is light," would no more dream of running the words into one conglomerate, unspaced in time to the ear, than he would set it up as a motto in a parish room with no more space to be seen between the last letter of one word and the first of the next. Once more, quiet experiment on the reader's part is recommended. Any proverb, uttered with no spacing, and then with various experimental spacings, will give a variety of results, which may be simulated on the written page as follows :

(i) Takecareofthepenceandthepoundswilltakecareofthemselves.
(ii) Takecareofthepence   andthepounds   willtake etc.
(iii) Take   care   ofthepence and thepounds etc.

Of these (i) gives a casual run-on effect, assuming that your hearer knows all about the sense of it, and only needs to have a button of memory touched and the meaning rushes into his mind faster than you can speak it. In such a case, perhaps the better course would be to say :

"Take care of the pence, etc."

It would be foolish to declaim it with all the care of a first communication. (ii) Gives another effect. The spacing of the two chief words exhorts the mind to focus attention. It is the way it would be spaced by a sententious uncle talking, perhaps, to a nephew on the receipt of a tip. (iii) Has more music in it by reason of the spacing of the primal monosyllables *take* and *care*:

One sometimes wishes that the natural spacing and the consequent rhythmic tendencies of literary speech—yes, and even of conversational speech—could be somehow conveyed by the letter-spacing and word-spacing on the page, thus:

T a k e   c a r e ofthep e n c e —
a n d thep o u n d s will t a k e   c a r e ofthems e l v e s.

But it could only in a very limited sense be communicative of the way to speak thoughts seen in writing; and it would have precisely the dangers that all mechanical indications of imaginative realities have. A stock length comes to be attached to a stock sign, as in the case of written crotchets and quavers, often with disastrous effect; for, as is obvious, actual music, written perhaps in 100 stock crotchets and 200 stock quavers, has itself no stock sizes. The sizes and shapes of a thousand quavers indeed vary, as do a thousand leaves of a tree.

Now in the use of all these five elements of spoken utterance, it is fairly easy to lay down one general principle ; they are all subject to the master-faculty of speaker or singer alike—the creative imagination itself. Behind every word uttered is an imaginative output ; though it be nearly *nil*, it is bound to be there. Let any sentence in the language be uttered by any man in the country, and his utterance will, as we say, "give him away" to perceiving hearers. Pitch, volume, length, speed and spacing will all conspire to communicate his mind, such as it is and wherever it is. There is literally "no sound without signification." The sound may signify mere apathy or egotism, instead of sympathy and common-sense, but it inevitably signifies. Every utterance, in speech or song, signifies, *whether the utterer will or not*. Of course a voice may be "put on," like a uniform, in deference to custom. Anyone may unconsciously acquire, by imitating men he admires, a uniform that is neither his nor originally theirs. A voice can be nobody's voice because it is everybody's in that line of life. Uniforms have their value, and possibly their virtue. It may be good for a man to don a coat that gives him a new sense of his oneness with his comrades, and reminds him of his own appointed littleness. In the same way, a parson often seems to *don* a voice. But a uniform must never be a disguise. Moreover, a uniform voice must be made to fit. It must not squeeze or contract the nature of the wearer. When words that matter are spoken naturally, every sentence, and all the elements of its utterance together conspire both to carry and to kindle creative imagination which lies behind it. Of course, accompanying facial expression, gesture, and mere posture, as well as all expressive elements, other than speech, combine to convey the total imaginative reaction of the speaker who is visible. But even unseen utterance is eloquent, and a blind listener, hearing a reader, can assess the man behind the voice. It is for this reason we advise speakers who study the elements of utterance, to merge all their ultimate thoughts on the subject into one general homely maxim : Take no care except for *what* you imagine, and *how* you imagine (as you speak), and the speech will take care of itself.

(2) Bearing in mind the naturalness of these five elements or dimensions of utterance and their common effect upon us, the reply to our second question (as to communal speech) will not be hard to find. The opportunities of studying the natural effects of utterance in chorus are few in the case of adults, more plentiful in the case of children. Men and women speaking together do not "let themselves go" as children do. But on rare occasions one may hear what may be called the real thing in this respect. We may take as a fair example of it the utterance of the Apostles' Creed by any conference of keen men—clerical or lay—when the individual (being surrounded by his own kind) is not shy of letting himself be natural, alive, and keen-eyed about it. On such occasions one may hear what may be called the corporate working of precisely the same five principles of utterance. In this corporate working at least two remarkable symptoms— one might almost say new factors—appear : these may be called *stimulus* and *caution*.

There is to be noticed an exhilarating fortifying of

individual utterance through the working of the natural laws of *contagion* and *momentum*. Naturally, if everyone round you is apparently of your mind and inclination, the obvious effect seems to be a reinforcement, both of your mind and your inclination. Acting and reacting, contagion brings momentum and momentum augments contagion.

The second apparent interaction is as important; but it acts more as a brake upon the engine of utterance than as an added energy. In the end, however, it seems greatly to enhance and intensify the whole. The principle of neighbourliness, referred to previously, at once creates individual efforts to ensure unanimity by every instantaneous and unconscious process of give-and-take. Voice will wait for voice here and there instinctively, so that key-words may be synchronized strongly and the line of utterance kept. Extremes (of pitch especially) among individual voices will be unconsciously cut down and attuned, so that the natural inflections, rhythms, speed, and, in a lesser degree, volume, take on disciplined limitations which individuals, speaking alone, would never need to regard.

The net result of these two apparently opposite tendencies is a more tempered, yet more glowing utterance. This combination is particularly happy in the case of Christian public worship, where neither increase of restraint alone, nor of warmth alone, would satisfy the need at the high moments, where—*e.g.*, in a a *Gloria*, *Kyrie*, or, above all, in a *Sursum Corda*—it is fitting that all worshippers should join in the utterance spontaneously and to the fullest possible extent.

(3) Our third question is perhaps the most crucial of those with which church music is concerned.

Musical utterance at its simplest, all the world over, resolves itself into some form of melody. Melody may perhaps fairly be defined as a succession of well-related sounds imaginatively welded into a unity. However rich the harmonic and orchestral texture, all music remains (in essence) melody, since it must give a succession of sounds, whether single or composite, that are related and heard in process. Our question is : Are the elements of simple melody in music so nearly like to those of utterance in melodious speech as to make congregational song a spontaneous vehicle of the spirit of worship itself ? The answer might be negative without depreciation. One can imagine their being closely akin and yet mutually intractable or incompatible when the vital needs of worship are at stake. One can imagine the speaking voice—both alone, as when a priest speaks, and in chorus, when congregations respond—proving capable of serving all purposes of spontaneous and direct utterance in worship ; music (*i.e.*, melody, both of a single voice or instrument and of many voices or instruments) being restricted to uses at certain moments before, between, during or after worship as an aid. But is there need for such restriction ? Can singing never be like glorified speech, the very vehicle of worship itself ? Cannot sung worship be as perfect as spoken ? Is not musical utterance, at moments, indeed the very best vehicle of public worship, just as spoken utterance is at other moments ? When the rubric says, " Then shall be said or sung," is it not saying, "Both are good; do the most fitting in every case"?

We search for the practical reply to this crucial question especially at the present time, because impossible musical things may be and are frequently asked of congregations (with all good intentions), while, conversely, golden chances to mobilize the spirit of worship in spontaneous and beautiful musical ways seem to be missed. To us it seems beyond doubt that melodic utterance of a simple and wholly fitting order can become as natural to a normal Christian assembly as corporate speech, and far more beautiful. History supports this view, for there is a vast corpus of Christian melody from Ambrosian times till today. But the history and the habits of a few centuries are too slender witnesses for so great a matter. Honest doubters who long to be worshippers may still say to us: "When your singing starts, worship stops." Our trustier witnesses are inherent and profound.

Let any doubting reader glance, not merely at the likeness, but at the obvious identity of the basic principles of utterance in speech and song:

> (a) Rise and fall of the tones prove vital to all melodic utterance;
>
> (b) The longs and shorts of the tones are vital to all rhythm;
>
> (c) *Volume* has precisely the same expressive significances and the same dangers as in speech;
>
> (d) The sensible obligations of *speed*
>
> and (e) of *spacing* are as inescapable in song as they are in speech.

And it is, furthermore, obvious that the imaginative control and uses of all five principles of utterance together result in what in melody is called inspired phrasing, and is needed to convey the innermost sense of melody as of speech. This is by no means to suggest that song adds nothing to speech; or that they in themselves are identical because their methods of utterance are identically conditioned. That would be like saying that a poet has no more to give than a politician, or a singer in Queen's Hall than a porter at Paddington. When the voice of a melodist rises a perfect fourth from C to F, it rises purposefully, for it is communicating a taste, a perception, a purpose, a thought, a design—call them any name you can find. When his voice rises from C to F sharp he is communicating a totally different taste, thought, apperception, or design. But when a mere speaker unconsciously raises his voice by one degree or the other, this is not so. Melody presupposes love of and deliberate choice of euphonies ; and a composer loves the various euphonies so profoundly, so energetically, that he loves them into a musical unity called a "tune."

From this it will appear that the vital question lies beyond the question of the identity of their principles of utterance—speech and song. We have to note with joy and hope that melody does all that speech does, and something more, and this " more " lies in the direction, not only of harmony and vision but of unanimity of thought and utterance, regulating and unifying the tones of voice chiefly as to pitch and rhythm.

All this looks very hopeful for corporate utterance in worship; and one would be inclined to expand the familiar rubric musically: "Then shall be said or sung, and always sung if possible." But this brings us with more fear than joy to the crucial question: Can it be done? If so, how and at what cost? Can the beauty of melody, the euphonious "something more" be had with no general loss of spontaneity? Better speech than song (all will agree) if song brings artificiality, self-consciousness and a host of other side-tracking drawbacks into public worship. Yet, in our deliberate judgment, the reply to this crucial question should be a far more eager, unequivocal "Yes" than is at present apparent in church music. True, we have a long way to go (as already hinted) before rhythmic melody is a recognized and practised mother-tongue of the imaginative boy and girl from earliest infancy. But we have also a long way to go before Christian manners are the recognized manners even of the Christian church. It is not enough to say that church melodies are a good alternative vehicle of worship. Today we should all be able to go at least one step further than that, and recognize fearlessly that when a minister calls out to his flock: "Praise ye the Lord," and they heartily reply: "The Lord's Name be praised"; still more when he cries: "Lift up your hearts," and they whole-heartedly reply: "We lift them up unto the Lord," there should be no place in Christendom where both could not rise to some simple strain of natural melody or chant, some "devout and solemn note" (as Cranmer's momentous letter to his King put it) that is wholly as natural as speech and far more beautiful, "as near as may be for every syllable a note."

If, then, it be true that a form of congregational rhythmic melody, wholly at one with the words uttered, is the most natural vehicle of corporate worship, it is equally true that it will fail if it is ill-rendered by any or all concerned. We may see that fervent utterance turns speech into primal song. But unanimity—that is, the desired result—will never be attained at the loss of spontaneity. And spontaneity can come into no language that is only half learnt! The conditions necessary for the attainment of this simpler and most natural of all church music in responding, hymning and chanting are willing culture and good custom, from the smallest village school to the largest public school and onwards.

But many a thrilling use of corporate melody or chant has been attained already. How to promote and extend the knowledge of this vital order of congregational music is a big problem, some practical aspects of which are considered in detail in the next chapter.

CHAPTER IV

WORDS SAID OR SUNG

PRESENT PROBLEMS OF UTTERANCE

"Most deere Philip, in that a man is the most worthy of all Creatures, a creature made like to God, by nature milde, of stature upright, provident, wise; of memory, witty; by reason, susceptible of Lawes and learning; by his Creator's great gift, farre preferred before all unreasonable creatures in al things, but specially in two, to wit, Speech and Reason; it follows that Ignorance in him is so much the fowler fault, by how much hee is more worthy than other Creatures. Now this as it is a fowle shame for all men, so for Schollers it is the fowlest disgrace: the course of whose life is or-dayned for this, that by living well they may shew others an example of good fashions, learning and honesty, encreasing fervent Faith in the people, and (which is their chiefest Office) by praising God in Hymnes and songs, stirring up devotion in the hearts of the faithfull."—ORNITHOPARCUS (from the dedication of his "Micrologus," Book III).

WE have now to approach ground made difficult by three facts. There are culpable shortcomings to be pointed out, in musicians and their associates, and it is thankless work to deal with faults. But there are, when these are removed, thrilling possibilities of advance along simple and quite attainable lines. There is a general absence of awareness of the true nature both of the faults and the possibilities. The havoc worked by the faults is now perceptible; and hardly less clear is the way in which keenness can dispel them and make way for splendid possibilities to become actualities, and that at incredibly short notice. We wish to help our readers to find, if they have not already found for themselves, quick, practical ways of realizing the truth in their own churches. "I went with my wife on Good Friday to church," said one of the noblest and most famous men of our time. "But the way they treated that glorious Psalm xxii. was so terrible, I *could* not go again !" . . . "How is it," a lady asked Dr. Corfe, "that your choir sings so beautifully in tune?" "Oh, it's against the rules at Christ Church to sing flat," was the reply. And is it not against every rule of Christendom that words in worship should be uttered other than keenly, clearly, mindfully, considerately of all worshippers and their full powers ? Whether said or sung, by one or by many, words—together with their attendant silences—are the chief vehicle of public worship. The whole question of their utterance, as it exists today, needs to be considered from a sternly practical angle.

Let us for the moment view the whole tract of audible utterance in any given service (from the first sound to the silence after the Blessing) as a varied and fruitful ground where purposeful emphasis will cause some words to stand out in strength and beauty, like features in a landscape, and others to be spoken with great quietude, whether speedy or deliberate.

At the outset it is obvious that the range of possibilities is very wide, and that all words used, whether said or sung by clergy, choir or congregation, should as obviously be the effectual and spontaneous carriers of the spirit of that worship. Let a service one hour long be imagined. Let us suppose that, from first to last, only 3,000 words are to be uttered, including all readings, exhortations, psalms, hymns, prayers, responses, and sermon ; and that of these words none are superfluous ; all are well related and chosen that they may together conspire into a unity. Clearly we must, for the moment, take perfection in the words of the service itself for granted. For our concern here is not with the actual words, but with their utterance ; and not with their utterance in any one particular (such as clarity, reverence, etc.), but with their due and moving delivery as a well-related whole. For hungry souls have come to this service, looking to be fed ; souls astray, searching for guidance.

Of course, to be practical is to acknowledge at once that all 3,000 words may be (and, indeed, often are) handicapped and even ruined at the outset by the absence of the rudimentary qualities just named—reverence, or the clarity which implies reverence. Apathy and cheap, slip-shod ways are calamitous to utterances of far less importance than those of public worship. They can ruin a fine service. But, again, it is well here to take for granted that the service in question is really Christian in that it is at bottom free from apathy ; and whether said or sung, loudly or softly, quickly or slowly, with or without the aid of agreed and thoughtful silences, it is at least meant to be perfectly reverent. Serviceable clearness in every word is therefore to be taken for granted from first to last. It is to be assumed that the mind of every priest, as of the humblest of his colleagues in the chancel, is imbued, not only with the love of God, but also with the working rule: "Love thy congregation as thyself." Nothing will ensure kindly clearness in all 3,000 words (whether said or sung) so instantly and unfailingly as will the memory of the needs of the rather deaf old worshipper at the west end. This primary consideration of clearness must be observed, and can now fortunately be physically achieved in the largest place of worship in the land. One vast cathedral, at least, has, by a simple system of microphones, made it possible for every word to be heard with ease at hitherto impossible distances, and in defiance of hitherto embarrassing echoes. In average churches it has of course always been possible, granted the neighbourly will behind it.

Having cleared our ground, the practical problem presents itself in two main aspects: (1) How is the question of what words are best said and what words are best sung in any given service to be determined? And (2) how are we best to cope with the general melodic shortcomings of average contemporary congregations? Of course, the two questions hang inseparably together. To give congregations more than they can sing on the one hand, or to deny them the chance to contribute "all they know how" on the other, is equally to mar the ideal service we have in mind. Let us look first at what may be called the "say or sing" problem—which is as deeply interesting as it is important. To take extremes first; could the Exhortation be sung? It could; but it is not difficult to realize the greater obligation to speak it with quiet deliberation.

Again : could the Venite be spoken ? Yes ; but it is convincingly easy to see that it cries out to be sung by every soul in the place. The truth seems to be that, of our 3,000 words, those that evoke thought (and they will be many) will need to be quietly uttered ; while those that crystallize or epitomize thought into an energy of longing (well known to us all by experience) are fewer and will need to be sung. In other words, they will need to be uttered with considered unanimity of enthusiasm ; this leads to the use of tones of regulated pitch, length and loudness, which, in turn, leads to melodic utterance at the intense points of worship, whether in response, chant or hymn. Our 3,000 words can be, and mostly are, servants of due thought and quiet reflection. But at high moments, words must and do become very like pinions for the heavenly aspiring mind as it rises. As the barometer of man's mind rises, so speech notoriously tends to transmute into song, into some form of music—rhythmic, melodious and, of necessity, ordered and unanimous. But now our second practical problem faces us. At such points no worshipper must be prevented from joining. Here comes a painful dilemma. When speech becomes inadequate it must give rise to song. Yet, if the mere act of trying to sing becomes a congregational impediment, or, worse than that, a ludicrous anticlimax, then better far fall back again upon speech as hearty and adequate as it can be. It is obviously useless to talk about "pinions" of the aspiring mind when some amiable but musically bedraggled congregation is thinking of nothing but the effort of trying to pick up a tune too high, or too hard, or (even if easy) too unfamiliar, and not printed in their book — "words only" edition,* and miserably small type at that! This unhappy state of things must, of course, cease. Undoubtedly it will cease in the long run, like all such scandalous apathy, at last shamed out of existence. But ought we to let it have a "long run" in this age? Read the piercing words of "Ornithoparcus" quoted above, written (in a treatise on music) to his "most deere Philip" five hundred years ago. Complacent apathy and tolerated "ignorance" are our unbearable impediments; and in this case (if we are "schollers" as well as "calling ourselves Christians") it is indeed our present-day "fowlest disgrace." Our readers will be ready to bear with some vehemence here. When English infants, in every infant-school and kindergarten, are at last taught to read and write their own small tunes on the five-line stave as easily as they read or write a nursery rhyme; when our public schools possess their first and second orchestras as surely as their first and second cricket elevens, then melody will be known for the natural "mother-tongue" it is—as easy to learn as it is enjoyable to practise; incidentally, vapid melody will be at a greater discount, and noble tunes more commonly recognized and used. Ordinary congregations of men and women of good-will will then know how to use that mother-tongue to good purpose. At present they would most of them freely admit that,

* "Words only" editions of all our Hymnals are still printed by the million as we write, for the sake of cheapness, whereas if the inclusion of the bare melodies could be made the rule instead of the exception, the power to read melody would the quicker be a nationally accomplished fact.

though they are ready to worship like men, they are only able to sing like untutored babes, owing to their negligible musical education. To such it will be no offence if we are obliged momentarily to give such advice as might be offered to children. And, however lamentable the present shortcomings may be, it is good to reflect that there can scarcely be a reader who has not on occasion heard both spoken and sung words in Christian worship rise suddenly to thrilling splendour. At our public schools, for example, let the boys but get a tune within their compass that rises and falls as they seem intuitively to know it ought, and the miracle happens. It is all the sadder, of course, to recall that the very same boys may, the very next day, fall back into slovenliness and lifelessness, never reflecting (as they would in the playground) that such school-slackness is simply "not the thing." Some day (may we not believe?) all these shortcomings and apathies will be "simply not the thing" anywhere in Christendom.

We may now revert to our model service and to our picture of a tract of utterance in an hour's public worship, along which all the varied virtues of strong, sincere, worshipful utterance now to be noted will tend to spring up of themselves, provided the enthusiasm is there, and the words to be said or sung, singly or together, be aptly chosen for present-day uses. We will try to keep closely to the practical considerations, to be discussed in more homely details later.

Strong enthusiasm makes for clear speaking as well as strong singing, and these have, first and foremost, an "edge" upon them. When speech or song has more

and more intelligently related values, it tends to grow
not only clearer and more emphatic; it tends to give a
chorus of voices verbal *unanimity*, and what may be
called *unitonality* too. For an example of this kind of
spontaneous fervour in ordinary life, one only need go
to any lively meeting of university students. The
"gods" are usually fervent. They "*want*" something.
A speedy word is sent round; and in a few seconds you
may hear a thunderous shout: "*We want* SO-AND-SO!"
It will sound something like this:

It is all unrehearsed. Nobody is needed to conduct it.
Yet the rhythm is generally strikingly precise. Furthermore, the voices, by common and unstudied consent,
steady themselves on an approximate unitone, unconsciously imposed upon the team by its more dominant
members (even two eager ones can establish a tone). The
rise and fall on "SO-AND-SO" (or whatever the specific
demand may be) is more or less standardized, being dictated by the chief words and by the high spirits of the
people who set the demand going. In fact, the melody,
unconsciously extemporized, has generally a moving
quality about it, a youthful glory of its own that well
may be the envy of those of us who long to have a
chance, before we die, to hear the Christian Church
everywhere cry out its far more urgent WE WANT TO
PRAISE, or WE WANT TO BELIEVE, or WE WANT TO PRAY,
with like unanimity and unashamed heartiness, yet with
no loss of public decorum or violation of the due reti-

cence of the worshipper. This brings us face to face with
the great range of devout utterance from the quietest
Kyrie to the most voluminous *Gloria*. For, though apathy
can kill a service, reticence is a Christian attribute that
intensifies its utterances. Nothing is more moving in
speech (whether of one or many) than the burning control of utterances dictated by strong feeling. Are these
the attributes in today's customary corporate utterance
of the Lord's Prayer, the Creed and the Gloria? Bless-
ings on those parish priests who set themselves to lead
the congregation into a reverently unified, hearty and
intelligent utterance of these things! But so elementary
is the present failure to do this on both sides—clerical
and lay—that the instructions now to be given must
read rather like talk to schoolboys. Here they are:

(1) *No minister must disregard the utterances of his
congregation.* It seems as offensive to tell a minister to
consider and wait for his people, and not to go on by
himself regardless of consequences, as it would be to
tell an engine-driver or guard not to proceed regardless
of passengers. Yet this has, apparently, to be newly
laid down today as an unbreakable law of congregational worship! It is unbearable that any priest should
wilfully go forward with, for example, the words
"and in-earth-peace-goodwill-towards-men-We-praise-
thee-we-bless-thee-we-worship-thee-we-glorify-thee-
we-give-thanks-to-thee-for-thy-great-glory" at his own,
often cursory speed, regardless of what, and how much,
the congregation are hearing, and how they are faring
and following. How can a too tolerant Church be
brought to realise and end this worse than folly?

(2) *No congregation must fail to go with their minister and choir.* On this side also it may seem as offensive to an intelligent English congregation to be told it is their task to "jump into the train" of speech or song. They are to *get into* the Gloria, with their minister, and identify themselves keenly and carefully with their fellow-worshippers in the words uttered. Again, to say this at all should be as obvious a superfluity as it would be to tell the passengers to get into a train before the whistle sounds, and not linger about the platform.

Let us tabulate a few common-place bye-laws in the light of common-sense and, incidentally, of Christian charity :

> (i.) Where the minister's utterance cannot possibly be heard by the whole congregation, let "mediators" be stationed at a point where they can hear and keep with him, and where the main congregation can hear and keep with them (the mediating voices).

Specially alert members of a choir, musical servers, young "cantors," ex-choirboys who count it an honour to continue to serve their church and ministers in such a way after their voices have broken, may be particularly helpful in this connection.

> (ii.) Where the minister can make his voice audible to all, he must obviously think of the deafest and dullest members of the congregation placed furthest from him, and adapt his speed, spacing, tones and volume of tone *to their needs*. His task is to gather *all* into the utterance. The quick must mindfully regard the "slowest battalions."

(iii.) Where the minister can be heard by all, those
nearest to him should still make it their
special care to help him by alert unanimity
to gather up the more distant voices into
the general stream.

(iv.) *Actual Speed and Spacing.* These seem by far
the most important factors, and the golden
rule about them is apparently this : Let the
speed be always the *speed of the thought behind the words* ; and let the spacing be such as
gives room for each thought to be completed
without breaking the thread of the whole.

This last rule is no bye-law. It seems rather of the
nature of an unchanging principle. To take the quotation
from the Gloria given above, if the speed and spacing be
regulated according to the above rule, and spelt out in
musical notation, it might approximate to the following:

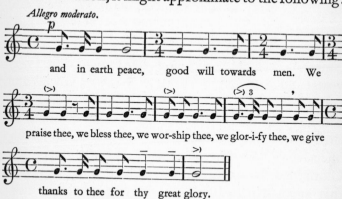

Whether spoken or sung the accents here given would
be quite naturally but never literally or unalterably observed, and the more natural they are the more they
will tend to pick up the heedless and distant souls in

the congregation and give the needed touch of strength to the whole utterance.

> (v.) Every congregational utterance should gather and use its own natural momentum, and this momentum should reach its maximum at the peak, or summit, of the utterance.

This is more a statement of fact than a rule, since it cannot but happen in every vital utterance. It should be noticed that momentum does not mean volume. The last sentence of the creed, for example, might be both the strongest and softest, the tone being subdued by the very strength of the worship.

> (vi.) Choirs should help congregations, and congregations should help themselves (those of strong purpose giving the lead) to give every syllable of every word clearness and its own right shape and size for carrying its meaning and falling into its place.

This rule includes the careful differentiation of every vowel and every consonant from its fellow-vowels and fellow-consonants. A blasé uniformity of vowel-sound, and a weak, flaccid style of consonant, common in tired colloquial speaking, are obviously intolerably offensive in such utterances as the Lord's Prayer, the Gloria and the Creed. But a warning must be added that aggressive clearness on the part of single worshippers, with however pious an intention, is a flaw in congregational utterance.

Clearness and care in speed must ultimately be, not individual, but corporate, and, in the initial stages of attaining this end, the keenest spirits must be the most intensely tactful in utterance themselves.

Much could be added to the above six suggested rulings, without discounting them in the minds of those most anxious to dispel the discouraging apathy today. What would the clergy who rattle through the most profound petitions *presto*, day after day, say to any musician who rattled *presto* through the first movement of the "Moonlight" Sonata? But even the poor, single-sentence prayer of the publican can be more important to men at worship than a million "Moonlight" Sonatas. What has come to pass in this our needy and enlightened age, that, in the highest places of worship in the land, we have to listen, Sunday after Sunday, to such a thoughtless enormity as the following:

Al-migh-ty God, un-to whom all hearts be o-pen, all de-sires known.

Ruling (iii.) above only suggests that in this splendid and solemn preparatory prayer, every communicant present shall be given *reasonable time* to think and mean the succession of thoughts contained in it with becoming reverence:

   (*a*) That God is all might;

   (*b*) That there is not a heart of a single inhabitant of the globe shut to Him;

   (*c*) That all desires of all men are known to Him.

Time is of the essence of the contract here in exactly the same way in which it is essential for Beethoven to think such calm thoughts as these:

Let the reader play this *presto*, and observe the effect on Beethoven disciples, or on himself if he have discernment. That thoughtless, unloving utterances of momentous prayers are to be heard daily on the lips of leaders forces upon us the question: Is the evil due to repetition? Is it, perhaps, repetition beyond absorption-point which works this kind of havoc with clerical minds? Yet, repetition is good! It is, perhaps, only good when it still can be identified with the spirit and effort of *perfecting*. Any other repetition than that which amplifies the meaning of the words must, it would seem, fall under the withering reproof of Christ Himself, as *"vain."*

We may now turn from this painfully rudimentary table of hints to the consideration of their application to, and effect upon, our service as a whole. For the effort to give the fitting and most adequate utterance to every one of our 3,000 words, whether by clergy, choir or congregation, would result in something far more important, namely the vital effort duly to relate word to word into a service of refreshing proportions and unity, without monotony and without excess.

One of the wisest, most sympathetic, and saintly critics, hearing a full cathedral service at the Temple Church one Sunday morning, found it very beautiful but "full of climaxes." A particularly fine psalm (for example, ciii.) was in itself a spiritual climax, the Te

Deum was a climax; so were the Benedictus, the anthem, the Nicene Creed and the triumphant hymn. This was a clearly flagrant case of excess of musical zeal, giving glowing settings to great words regardless of the powers of the worshipper to absorb them. We all are painfully familiar with the opposite abuse, when the whole tract of utterance is flat country. Mr. Gladstone once reproved the easy critic of the easy-going service when he said he had never heard a sermon with no point of interest in it; but, he added, he was bound to say it was often only the text!

When a three-syllabled word is uttered, the point is not merely that all three syllables should be vitally and clearly uttered, but that their proportions should be so intelligently right as to move us. Think of the word "commandment," for example, without the challenging swing of the voice into the second syllable. It becomes something less than itself if every syllable is uttered as of equal importance. (Let the reader try it.) Similarly, on the most comprehensive scale possible, our interest in this chapter is not merely that those imagined 3,000 words should be workmanlike, but perfectly proportioned to carry the spirit of the service and recreate the worshippers. Authorities in each church must look to it that the words that are better said should not be sung; those that are better sung must not be said; for this would be short-coming. Furthermore, those that are best said or sung slowly, or softly, or speedily, or loudly, must all fall into their places in our general tract of utterance, and the words that form the fitting climax of the service must receive their due regard. And this is not really so hard a matter. All can enter into it. It needs only thought and ready control of personal inclinations for the good of the whole. It is, moreover, intensely interesting and stimulating to those who study it. It can be made the deliberate subject of sermons, and one of the aims of the congregational practices that will be discussed in a later chapter.

To conclude, let us imagine this natural voice of worship at work, and watch analytically its obedience to the natural rules of the game as we have tried to describe them in this and the previous chapter. For this purpose we must think of the speaking and singing voice as one. Think of any well-known psalm—take, for example, Psalm ciii.—as being sincerely spoken (by one or many), or in a kind of chant wonderfully suited to the voice as it works to get the whole spirit of the psalm through. Watch the voice in the first verse:

"Praise the Lord, O my soul :
    and all that is within me praise His holy Name."

It would naturally tend to keep every rule named in Chapter IV. as to the rise and fall, the long and short, the strong and weak of the utterance. Thus (a) it would naturally rise in the first verse on the significant word "*all* that is within me"; (b) it would lengthen such "carrying" syllables as *praise*, *Lord*, *soul*, and relatively shorten the little syllables round them; (c) it would give volume to all these forthright words and verses generally, and proceed to lessen volume gradually as the psalm grows more con-

6

templative ; (d) it would speed up the ecstatic final verses, after having slowed down in the reflective verses beginning "the days of man are but as grass" ; (e) it would carefully space out the similes ("like as the east," etc., and "like as a father") in order to give the listener's responsive mind the needed time to swing over thoroughly into each profound comparison as it is made—and all of this quite unconsciously !

It is just such instant and spontaneous application of the various means of expression in detail that makes for eloquent phrasing. In such a phrase, for example, as :

"who saveth thy life from destruction,"

one can hear the pitch normally rise to the word *life*, then fall ; while the long and short, and strong and weak syllables would together produce some such natural rhythm—whether in speech or chant—as this :*

who sav - eth thy life from de - struc - tion.

But in the end, the whole technique of utterance would subconsciously bring to light the design of the psalm itself : its exuberant start, its deepening thought, its sorrowful reflections, and its final reckless ecstasy of trust and praise. The choir would discover strong,

* The reader cannot too carefully guard himself from reading these approximate note-values as a fixity to be literally observed. No mensural music ever survives such treatment ; much less can chanting or speech be held literally to any notational aid. The picture in notes is needed, only to help the mind to freedom and clear concepts. Given these, the voice will escape the common danger of turning notes into fetters.

ringing, swift utterance at the outset, still more at the end, with perhaps a natural *allargando* of the very last six words, while the intermediate verses would be markedly varied, quieter, lower, slower by turns.

In the case of an inspired and cultured reader this would all occur naturally and without premeditation or study. But the fact has to be faced that the indispensable condition of spontaneity is too often absent in the case of singing, because the boon of a mastered and unconsciously applied technique is far less frequent in the singer than in the speaker.

Indeed, when all is said, the crucial question will still recur: Can what happens naturally in the case of sincere reading, and that only after long unconscious practice, be acquired and become our ordinary use in corporate worship, even on the very simplest lines here suggested? Well, the only true answer to this recurrent question seems to us to be a persistent and faithful "*Yes*," but not at the expense of worship itself. Though it is true that present-day singing is a far less natural art than present-day speaking; though the singing instinct in man, woman and child has been badly damaged by the performing sense; yet the thrill of simple choral melody as an actual carrier of the rapture of worship beyond all speech has been, and can be attained by the humblest of folk. The process of making it the accepted thing through the whole country, indeed through the whole of Christendom, must needs be slow. Only very gradually will people come to sing as un-selfconsciously as they speak.

With all these things in mind, we would strongly

urge the reader to pursue his own line of thought and study of English as a vehicle of the creative mind, whether in worship or in anything else. But we wish to warn him beforehand that, while the general popular understanding of the simple principles of utterance discussed here is so urgently needed, it is but a preliminary ; and all that is written in this chapter should be read in order to be forgotten. For whether in speech or song it is notoriously fatal to be thinking of one's voice or its effect. Yet the five points must be so assimilated as to be forgettable. Like bodily nourishment, they have to be "inwardly digested." Both agreed speech and agreeable song can, indeed, attain in action to a molten amalgam of all factors of eloquence, but only when all are mastered and none remembered.

Only inspiration can use and forge technique as it chooses ; and inspiration comes, not by careful tuition, but by care-free intuition. We would remind the reader of Sir Walter Parratt's remark to a singing bird : "Ah, my little dear, you wouldn't sing like that if you'd been taught !" Yet this luminous quip of a great teacher would only darken counsel if his fellow-teachers took it to mean "away with your teaching !" It can only mean that all good singing lies on the further side of the forgotten pains of learning. Physically, we are as free-born singers as the birds. Spiritually, we must continually take pains to attain freedom. That it is gloriously worth it in this matter of worship-music, all must agree.

PART II

PRACTICAL TEAM WORK

"SHARING each other's tastes for good things, and
therefore competing with one another, we have devised
a system of distribution of our activities. . . . Dis-
interestedness is a feature present in art as well as in
virtue. . . . Fine art unites men into society in respect
of production, virtue unites them so in respect of
practice. . . ."—S. ALEXANDER: *Beauty and other
Forms of Value*.

CHAPTER V

THE TEAM SPIRIT

"Gird yourselves with humility to serve one another."—St. PETER.

THE title of this chapter describes in a brief and homely way the first necessity of all good choral work, from the simplest to the most elaborate. It is borrowed from sport, because the games field provides the best illustration of the fact that in any kind of communal activity unselfish co-operation counts for more than brilliant individualism. This is true even of a pair at tennis, as it is of a couple playing or singing duets ; it is immeasurably truer of a football team and of a choral society ; and the principle applies above all to a church choir, whose organization and work must take account of certain non-musical conditions. The church choir is, in fact, a choral body *sui generis*, for reasons that are, we think, worth examination, because they bear on the most vital aspects of the choir's work.

The qualifications for membership of a choral society are purely musical, and rightly so ; whereas entry to a church choir is (or ought to be) via membership of the church. Such a term as "religious test" is unpopular today. Very well ; let us avoid it and put the case in a way that is as inoffensive as it is uncompromising. The church choir is a section of church workers drawn from the congregation, like any other voluntary church organization ; and practising membership of the church ought to be as naturally assumed in the case of a church singer as of a church parish councillor, a lay reader, or a district visitor. A church choir is therefore not an independent organization, but a small section of the congregation—we might call it an executive committee in the most literal sense, with the choirmaster as chairman—charged with the musical interests of the congregation. The method by which a choir will fulfil that charge varies widely in accordance with the local needs and traditions, the wish of the incumbent and congregation, or the policy of the choirmaster arrived at after consultation with the incumbent. A poorly equipped choir may find itself highly tried by the demands made on it ; on the other hand, a highly efficient or ambitious choir may be called on to limit its activities to a point far below its attainments and desires. Herein lies a fundamental difference between a church choir and a choral society—a difference so obvious that it needs to be pointed out from time to time. A choral society's performances are limited only by the musical ability of its average member : those of a church choir must always be governed by a number of conditions that apply to no other performing body, and chief among these is the factor (again obvious, and almost universally ignored) that the hearers are not an audience, but a gathering of fellow-worshippers whose primary interest in the proceedings is not musical. Indeed, to some of those present any music that is not simple may be a distraction rather than a devotional stimulus. Nor can this minority be ruled out of the discussion on the ground that it consists of a handful of admittedly unmusical people, for it is an easily verifiable fact that the preference of this minority is shared by many trained musicians. That the extremes of musical and non-musical folk may thus hold the same view on a musical question is a fact—and a significant one—that is too rarely considered by choirs and choirmasters.

This difference between a choral society and a church choir being granted—that the former is a purely musical organization singing to an audience interested in choral music, and the latter a small body of lay-workers deputed to lead their fellow-worshippers in praise and to beautify the service further, so far as their skill allows and time permits—this difference granted, it follows that church choir membership demands an unusual degree of unselfish co-operation. And by co-operation we mean not merely a pulling together among the members themselves, but something more difficult and vital : the choir must be united in aim and spirit with the clergy and congregation.

Now union, as the proverb says, is strength ; and to the question "Why ?" the reply is as obvious as the proverb. But is it not equally true that the strength is the result not only of common aim, but of common sacrifice as well ? No collection of individuals can combine without some concession on the part of every member. Let us see how this applies to our church choral team.

Votes of thanks to a voluntary choir invariably lay stress on the time the members willingly give to the practices. But time is not the hardest thing to sacrifice : church music ought to cost singers more than that.

The musical needs of the church may call for sacrifice in regard to likes and dislikes ; attractive and familiar things may have to be dropped in favour of some that are at first (perhaps even permanently) unattractive. The giving of an hour a week is a trifling sacrifice in comparison with the loyal undertaking of an uncongenial task. A choir that holds together cheerfully during an unpopular change of regime is exemplifying team spirit of the highest type.

This kind of self-denial is not confined to the choir : the congregation may be no less highly tried. The giving up of a popular bad hymn-tune in favour of a good new one may, to the detached observer, seem but a trifle: experience often shows it to be what Mr. Chesterton would call a Tremendous Trifle. On the other hand, zealous church music reformers may have to be content to make haste slowly in raising the standard of taste in choir and people. Old associations inevitably count for much in any kind of communal music ; to disregard such associations—even more to scoff at them—is to rouse a spirit of opposition that may tend to establish the "old favourite" even more strongly. It is a far from rare experience to find a congregation split asunder over the choice of a hymn-book, or even of a solitary tune. A disaster of this kind points to a lack of tact on the official side, or of reasonableness in the congregation ; and it is a regrettable probability that both parties will be concerned less with the doctrinal soundness or the spiritual value of the hymns than with the character or quality of the tunes to which they are sung.

*   *   *   *   *

Of the musical and non-musical aspects of the team spirit, we have dealt with the latter first because it is usually the less regarded of the two, despite its fundamental importance. (The give-and-take demands of choral singing are far more easily met, if only for the reason that their urgency is more apparent.)

As this book is not a musical primer, but rather an attempt at a considered statement of aims and ideals, we do not propose to deal exhaustively with the technical side of choir training, especially as the ground is already well covered by textbooks, particulars of which will be found in the bibliography. Instead, we choose for discussion a factor that is usually passed over, either because its importance is too little realized, or because it is taken for granted. This factor is listening; and we enlarge the term into the listening habit, because listening on demand, so to speak, is a cure, whereas listening by habit is a preventative.

Elsewhere in this book we summarize such purely vocal requirements as blend, balance, intonation, and ensemble into an alliterative trinity of activities—toning, tuning and timing.

They are attainable only through listening: the singer must listen to himself, to his fellows, and to the accompaniment. To himself: a less natural process than it may seem to be. Every teacher and student of solo singing knows that the person least aware of the quality and character of tone being produced is the singer himself. His is more than a case of being too near the instrument, or even of being the instrument itself, for the instrument is inside him; he is a mere container. That is why the student begins by taking the word of his teacher as to whether he is producing good tone; he develops the habit of listening acutely to himself; he observes the physical sensations that are both cause and effect of the varied qualities of tone comprised in his voice; and he ends by being able to play on this hidden and most sensitive of all instruments with the ease and resourcefulness of a pianist or violinist. Now, this constant listening and testing is well within the power of the average choir-singer, with, of course, the co-operation of the choirmaster. Any keen and competent choir-trainer who has had long experience of teaching boys of the ordinary parish church choir type will bear witness as to the readiness with which they will develop a listening faculty that begins with inculcated habit and ends by being instinctive and subconscious. The high standard of the best English boy trebles is ample proof of what can be done in this way with material that is available, in great or small measure, in every centre of population.

The adult untrained singer is a more difficult proposition: he starts, as a rule, handicapped by bad vocal habits, whereas the boy begins with a clean slate; and the more highly developed mentality of the grown-up may be a hindrance rather than a help because—like the adult voice itself—it is more "set," and less elastic and responsive than that of the boy. Nevertheless, that average untrained adults are capable of being developed into capital chorus singers is proved over and over again at Competition Festivals, the best results often being achieved by choirs from villages and small towns where a few years previously a choral society did not exist. There is a recent case on record where the village in question not only had had no choral society, but where the villagers broke into astonished laughter when their first conductor produced a stick for conducting. They had never seen one ! But before their second year was out, they had taken two first prizes and the Wakefield Medallion at their county festival. What is done in all parts of the country by these choral societies ought to be done by the church choirs that draw their material from the same source. That it is *not* done is patent.

Nor will it be done until the church choirmaster ceases to confine his attention to the boys in regard to vocal training and sight-singing. Let the difficulties be granted : the men are present at one weekly practice, whereas the boys are usually present at several ; the practice attended by the men is actually a rehearsal for the ensuing Sunday rather than a practice at which fundamentals and general principles can receive attention ; and the presence of the boys precludes special work for the men, partly because it involves dangerous inactivity for the boys, and even more because the feelings of the men have to be considered : they naturally object to their deficiencies being exposed before youngsters. It is rarely possible to obtain the presence of the men for an extra practice, even if the choirmaster can spare the time ; but a plan that, from personal experience, we know to be successful is the tacking on of even a quarter of an hour extra for the men at the end of the full practice. It will usually be found that, having reserved the evening for choir-work, they will not grudge this extra period. (Occasionally, when the Sunday work is well in hand, the full practice may well be shortened for the benefit of the men's training.) In this weekly quarter of an hour a great deal of valuable work may be done by a choirmaster who is able to deal with elementary matters in an interesting and practical way.

The two subjects that should be given first place in a men's practice are voice-production and sight-reading. It must be said frankly that there is a tendency, in church choir and choral society alike, to shirk these subjects, on the ground that singers dislike them. But is not the real reason more often the inability of the teacher himself? Few choirmasters have themselves received any vocal training since their childhood: the fundamentals of singing are alike for all voices, but there are difficulties in the use of the adult voice that can be overcome only by a trained adult teacher. The necessary preparation need be neither long nor costly: a couple of terms with a good teacher will enable a choirmaster to show his basses how to "cover" the tone in order to produce musical and expressive top notes instead of a shout, and to demonstrate to his tenors the use of the light or "head" register. He may help himself, too, by studying a few of the many simple practical books on the subject (included in the bibliography). Nor can the choirmaster, amateur or professional, afford to neglect the valuable aid offered by the admirable choir-training examinations of the Royal College of Organists. There are two grades, one for the non-diplomées of the College—a scheme specially designed for the amateur and semi-professional—and a more exacting one for those who hold the Associate and Fellowship diplomas. Here it may be said in passing that the standard of choir-training will be greatly improved when incumbents, and others who are responsible for filling appointments, show a preference for the holders of the College Choir-Training Certificate. A good organ player is an acquisition, but a good choir-trainer is a treasure, even though he be only a moderate hand at the keyboard ; for, when all is said, the congregation may easily escape voluntaries by a punctual arrival and an expeditious departure, whereas the results of bad choir-training have to be endured.

In addition to the R.C.O. choir-training examinations there are frequent courses in the subject at the headquarters of the School of English Church Music (St. Nicolas College, Chislehurst) ; and in most dioceses there is a Church Music Committee under whose auspices summer schools and other educational gatherings are held. Never, in fact, had choirmasters so many facilities for learning their job cheaply and pleasantly as they have today. But in the long run, we repeat, the responsibility rests on incumbents and church councils. It is their plain duty to put first things first by engaging a choirmaster and organist rather than an organist and choirmaster ; to insist, when filling an appointment, on (a) unequivocal testimony to the applicant's choir-training ability ; or (b) the possession of an R.C.O. certificate, or evidence of attendance at a School of English Church Music training course. In cases when a promising organist is already in office, they should enable him to take advantage of facilities for improving himself as a choirmaster, by granting occasional leave of absence, adding, if necessary, such small financial aid as may be called for.

Returning to the problem of the training of the choirmen, let it be assumed that no special practice for their benefit is possible, or that the choirmaster is unable to give them instruction on the purely vocal side. Even in these discouraging circumstances much may be done where there is goodwill backed up by the common-sensible and practical qualities that are lumped together in the term gumption. A good deal of voice-training may be done by simple and indirect means that need little skill on the part of the teacher, and that have the further advantage of being palatable to men who would shy at the term "voice-production." Thus, even the roughest voices shed a good deal of their crudity if the choirmaster asks for (and sees that he gets) plenty of soft and *mezzo-forte* unaccompanied singing at the weekly practice ; and the custom of singing unaccompanied at least one verse or hymn at every service will speedily bring about an all-round improvement besides adding a touch of variety. A familiar hymn-tune or chant, or a phrase of it—even a single chord—can be used as a medium for practising blend, balance, breathing (sustaining evenly for a given number of beats after a quiet deep intake of breath), and articulation (simple sentences, some of them chosen or invented to overcome faults and to develop virtues ; counting at varying speeds is particularly useful, as it constitutes a multiple exercise—intonation, blend, balance, quality of tone, articulation — and the counting serves to register the breath-control); add power contrast and nuance ($\leq\ \geq$), and a common chord may be made an attractive and easy vehicle for development of many of the fundamentals of choralism. New chants and hymn tunes can be made valuable means of developing sight-singing and good tone. Instead of a part being played over and imitated, parrot-wise, by the singers, it should be *read*, no matter how much stumbling occurs ; and if new and unfamiliar chants and hymns are hummed and vocalized, all vowels being used in turn, sometimes preceded by a consonant chosen with a special object (*t* and *d* for tongue, *p* and *m* for lips, *n* for nasal resonance, and so on), the music will be assimilated and the voices improved rapidly. Humming is especially valuable as a cure for bad tone, throatiness and forcing ; good *free* humming (*i.e.*, with the facial muscles relaxed as in the involuntary humming expressive of a contented mind) is, in fact, one of the safest and best of all exercises ; and though simple and fundamental, it can always be resorted to with profit and pleasure.

There is general agreement amongst prominent choral trainers, especially in the most important North of England centres of choralism, as to the value of even a slight knowledge of tonic solfa as a basis for sight-reading. Prejudice against the system still exists in some academic quarters, especially among musicians who are primarily instrumentalists ; and their objections are in part due to the attitude of solfa extremists who

7

regard the method as an end in itself rather than as
(1) a quick and easy means of learning to read, invaluable in circles where time is limited, and (2) as a
stepping-stone to intelligent use of the staff notation,
the system which has three irrefutable claims : (*a*) it is
historic, (*b*) its usage being practically universal, it
constitutes the nearest approach to a world-language,
and (*c*) it is the only notation in which the whole of the
musical repertory is expressed.

The sight-reading problem is one that must be faced,
for the choral situation today is anomalous. There is
probably more widely diffused choralism than ever
before, yet the level of sight-singing is perilously low.
We say "perilously" because of our conviction that the
splendid choral work now being done in rural and
other small centres cannot be fully developed—much
of it, indeed, will probably cease—unless the standard
of sight-reading is considerably raised. It is no exagger-
ation to say that a very large proportion of the members
of choirs of all kinds are musically illiterate ; the older
members of church choirs and choral societies are (we
hear from many quarters) inclined to shy at sight-
reading classes ; the younger members, many of whom
acquired the rudiments of tonic solfa in their school-
days, find little opportunity of developing their knowledge of the system, still less of using it as a basis for
staff-reading. The future of choralism is with these
young members : can they be expected in this age of
speed and many counter-attractions to retain their
interest in choral work when the weekly practice consists of tedious repetition of a few part-songs, learned

mainly by ear? Or of church choirs, by whom even a new hymn-tune has to be picked up, part by part, after countless playings over? Reading that depends over-much on "ear" is an expensive makeshift—expensive in time and labour and in subsequent mistakes in per-formance, for the results are rarely safe: the mastery of a tricky passage demands a conscious use of mind and musicianship rather than of instinct, and these faculties must work through a ready visual grasp of notation. Hence the truth of the doggerel summary: "Ear-reading is dear reading; sight-reading is right reading."

The explanation of the low standard of music-reading in church choirs is simple. The bulk of the repertory is published in staff-notation only; the staff is difficult to teach to those who come fresh to it in adult years; even adults who know the staff through previous experience as pianists find it by no means easy to sing from. (On keyboard instruments the notes are ready-made, and all intervals and combinations of sounds are equally easy; singers have to make their own notes, and to the inexperienced there are few easy intervals outside scale passages and the notes of the common chord.)

The sight-reading difficulty is accentuated by the fact that the choir members who need help the most are those whose practice-time is least—the adults. It is often said that boys need no instruction in sight-reading: they acquire the gift naturally. A truer state-ment of the case is that boys learn to read quickly (by association of signs seen with the sounds heard) in spite of the lack of knowledge or specific instruction, and because of advantages not possessed by their adult colleagues. They are quick in the uptake ; the mere fact that they are schoolboys as well as choristers ensures a degree of receptivity denied to grown-ups whose minds and habits are set, and whose interests lie in a hundred other directions ; both the imitative faculty and the memory are at their best in childhood ; and, above all, as the treble part usually consists of the tune, it is more easily "picked up" than any other part. Even the fact of its being the top part counts for a good deal, as is proved when boys are called on to sing a second treble part of fair difficulty. On the whole, however, if time is limited, choirboys can get along pretty well without much sight-reading practice, though the wise choir-master will take advantage of the knowledge of tonic solfa they acquire at school ; and he will use it especially in the overcoming of difficult intervals and changes of key. One element in reading, however, should always be taught to boys : time-values of notes and rests. Tunes may be picked up ; time must be taught. Right notes sung out of time become wrong, and in a way that is often disastrous. The use of such a book on the elements as "The Little Choir Book," by Thomas Curry (Novello, 1½d.), will save much labour and temper all round ; and a very practical and attractive way of getting over the difficulty is a set of scale exercises by Walter S. Vale, in which all the most commonly used note-values and rests are employed. It is published by the Faith Press, and costs a mere penny. The habit of beating time by a slight movement of the hand should also be encouraged.

Choirmasters and choirs alike are naturally reluctant to grapple with the problem—ostensibly on the ground of lack of time. Yet, met aright, the difficulty can be overcome at small expense of labour and time. "There is no doubt," says Dr. W. G. Whittaker (one of the many music educationists who are also tonic solfa enthusiasts),

> "that the best way of teaching the staff, which ought to be the object before every worker in the singing-class field, is through solfa, using thoroughly its methods and as much solfa notation as is necessary to gain the ultimate goal. . . . Every staff step should be preceded by its equivalent in solfa. . . . It is a mistake to postpone staff notation until singers are able to read fluently in solfa. . . . Many teachers imagine that when they teach *facts* about staff notation they are teaching their class to sing. This shows misunderstanding of the very basic principles of sight-singing. The knowledge that a certain line is E, that a certain sign is a crotchet, is of no more value in sight-singing than the theory of relativity. The principle enunciated by John Curwen, 'Teach the thing before the sign, the sound before the notation,' is a fundamental law. The less theory that is taught the better; there should be only the barest minimum, and that should be introduced only when practical work has reached a stage which demands it. A fact which is not used frequently is quickly forgotten and time spent over it is wasted. First teach your class to *read*, and *then* to know a few simple facts about notation."*

* "Class Singing," by W. G. Whittaker (Oxford University Press).

Reading first, facts later : how wild the idea sounds ! Yet it is worth a trial by those who have drudged away at the names of the notes on the lines and spaces, the functions of the sharp, flat, and natural, and so forth ; only to find that, after all, the singers continue to guess rather than read, the musically endowed guessing well, the others . . .

"The thing before the sign, the sound before the notation :" experience will prove this to be an astonishingly easy process. Every person not tone-deaf finds little difficulty in identifying and singing the notes of the common chord—*doh*, *me*, *soh*, *doh*—the framework of the scale on which most modern music is written. With a little practice these may be sung in any order and at varying pitches ; solfaing from the staff should then begin, any line or space being used for *doh*. The next step is vocalizing from the staff, *i.e.* singing the notes of the chord to a vowel sound instead of to the solfa names (*lah* is often used for such vocalizing, but as it is the name of a note, the plain vowel *ah* is better ; other vowels may be used with advantage, sometimes preceded by a consonant, *pah*, *nah*, and *mah* being especially useful). The framework of the scale having been thoroughly mastered, the filling-in may be done, the best order being *ray*, *te*, *fah*, *lah*. The sharpening or flattening of notes is easily taught by being dealt with first in solfa, mainly because the effect is suggested by the names : *fah* sharpened becomes *fe* ; *te* flattened is *taw*, and so on. Even these early stages of approach to the staff seem complicated when set forth on paper. Actually the process is simple. A skilled teacher can, in fact, lay the foundation of good reading by the use of no more elaborate apparatus than his hands—the left held up fanwise to represent the scale, the forefinger of the right used as a pointer. He would probably begin with two fingers, taking the little finger as *doh*, the next as *me*, with the space between for *ray*, adding the remaining fingers and thumb with their spaces one at a time. All the fingers and spaces in turn should be used for *doh*. The hand can then be used to represent the staff, the *doh* still being movable. This method is as old as the hills—as some hills, at least— for Guido d'Arezzo used the left hand in an even more elaborate way, each finger-joint representing a note, the result being analogous to the Tonic Solfa modulator.

For the average inexperienced teacher—especially if he be himself a beginner in solfa—there is an excellent set of little textbooks called "The Dual Notation Course," particulars of which are given in the bibliography. By the use of these, the teaching of solfa and staff proceeds simultaneously from the first.

We have dwelt at some length on this matter, because we are convinced that the future of choral singing in this country is largely bound up with it. A very large proportion of the finest choral music, sacred and secular, is compounded of simple passages that any normally intelligent person ought to be able to sing at sight. And, for the encouragement of the timid, we repeat that even a very slight knowledge of solfa is an invaluable aid to reading from the staff, especially if it be backed up by some familiarity with the "time-names." (These are a simple set of syllables that teach note-values through rhythm, just as solfa teaches the staff through a grasp of intervals and the relationship of the notes of the scale.)

Convinced by our first-hand acquaintance of the astonishing results obtained by use of the solfa system in teaching choralists of all sorts, from infants to adults with no previous musical training and with little time to spare, we end this chapter with a few facts designed to remove the anti-solfa prejudice that still exists among professional musicians.

First, we quote the opening paragraph of the eight-column article, "Tonic Solfa," in *Grove's Dictionary* (1928 edition):

> Tonic solfa is the name of a method of teaching sight-singing from a special form of notation which has had the most far-reaching effect in promoting popular choral singing throughout the British Isles.

So far from the system being opposed to the staff, it sets out to supply the best of approaches thereto. Staff notation is the growth of centuries, and, having developed slowly and simultaneously in many countries to meet all needs, it contains elements that are puzzling to the beginner. Admirably adapted for all comprehensive and instrumental purposes, it is difficult for singers in early practical stages, especially in chromatic and dissonant passages. Tonic solfa is an explanatory and, as such, a severely logical system, free from the difficulties of the staff, where explanatory processes are necessarily outgrown. (Chromatic passages, for instance, give very little trouble in solfa, owing to a principle of key-transition which, in effect, leads to the employment of only one key.)

Though the solfa system is less than a century old, it has a mediæval basis, its sound-names dating from about a thousand years ago. Here, in modern notation, is the plainsong hymn, "Ut queant laxis," written by Paulus Diaconus, about 770; a couple of centuries later Guido d'Arezzo, observing that the opening notes of the first six of its seven phrases made up the hexachord (the scale from C to A), adopted the syllables sung to these notes, and used them as names.

Ut que-ant lax - is *Re* - so-na - re fi - bris *Mi* .... ra ges - to - rum

Fa-mu-li tu - o-rum, *Sol* .... ve-pol-lu - ti *La*-bi - i re-a - tum,

San....cte Jo..an..nes.

Do was substituted for *Ut* in the seventeenth century, and adopted throughout Europe except in France, where *Ut* is still used. (The origin of the *Do* is doubtful; it is either the first syllable of *Dominus*, or of *Doni*, the name of an Italian musician.) At the end of the sixteenth century *Si* was adopted for the seventh note of the scale, being changed to *te* in 1835 by Miss Glover of Norwich, the originator of the system that was later perfected by the Rev. John Curwen, who changed *Sol* to *Soh*, and invented the modified names for sharps and flats.

The principle of key transition referred to above has for its basis the Movable *Doh*, examples of which may be found in any plainsong of fairly extended compass, the clef being placed on any one of the four lines, in order to avoid or minimize the use of leger lines. On this point *Grove* says :

> The syllables attributed to Guido were a notation, not of absolute pitch, but of tonic relation ; his *ut*, *re*, *mi*, etc., meaning sometimes

> and sometimes

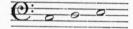

> and so on, according as the tonic changed its pitch ; and this ancient use of the syllables to represent, not fixed sounds, but the sounds of the scale, has been always of the greatest service in helping the singer, by association of name with melodic effect, to imagine the sound. The modern innovation of a "fixed Do" is one of the many symptoms (and effects) of the domination of instruments over voices in the world of modern music.

And an interesting footnote tells us that Sir John Herschel (whose musicianship has been forgotten owing to his fame as an astronomer) in an article entitled "Musical Scales" written for the *Quarterly Journal of Science* in 1868 said :

"I adhere throughout to the good old system of representing by Do, Re, Mi, Fa, etc., the scale of natural notes *in any key whatever*, taking *Do* for the keynote, whatever that may be, in opposition to the practice lately introduced (and soon, I hope, to be exploded), of taking *Do* to represent one fixed tone C—the greatest retrograde step, in my opinion, ever taken in teaching music, or any other branch of knowledge." (The "fixed Do" is the system preferred in France and Belgium, but has been definitely rejected in England.)

The conclusion of the matter is that the time and work so ungrudgingly given to church music by thousands of boys and men in parish church choirs can yield only half results (if even that) so long as they remain in a state of musical illiteracy. A choirman who is unable to read a simple passage at the first or second attempt ought to be regarded as an anomaly instead of a common object of the seashore ; and for the parson who says he is fond of music, and adds heartily (as if it were a matter for pride) that he doesn't know *a* from *b*, the word anomaly is too mild.

CHAPTER VI

LEADERSHIP AND DISCIPLINE

THESE are not so much musical matters, perhaps, as ethical ones that cannot be omitted from a book of this kind.

Loyalty and efficiency cannot be obtained without :

(*a*) Complete adherence to the appointed leader, coupled with

(*b*) Complete accessibility of the leader to the thoughts and suggestions, critical and otherwise, of the choir itself.

There is no such thing as a musical autocracy in a healthy choral team : the whole personnel is responsible. For every choral "building" has an architect : the composer. The builders are the singers, and the conductor a foreman-builder whose word at the moment of rendering must be unifying law. But it must be borne in mind that the builders are something more vital still : they are the very stones of the building, down to the humblest "one-note man." They are all *living* stones, singing with fitting will and mind : hence the perpetual need of freedom to tell the foreman how and what they feel about it. This means that good practices should have the soldierly touch of drill under command, plus the social touch of committee-work under a benignant chairman. The idea has often been achieved, and the results, so far as we know, have never failed, provided the social choirman does not cease to be soldierly, and the amenable leader never ceases to be commanding.

Some modern factories have a suggestion-box by means of which employees offer their ideas of improvement in administration. But, within bounds, all choristers may well make their thoughts known at the very moment they occur to them. Give choirboys the chance to suggest improvements in pointing of psalm verses or in *tempi* in anthems, and they will show both enthusiasm and sense in a high degree, with what has been called "respectful familiarity," often to the great increase of interest among the whole choir. The grown-ups are less willing to risk being right or wrong. This is unfortunate, because it is usually this department of the choir that needs most the vitalizing effect of an occasional discussion of methods. In any case it may safely be remembered that while agreed leadership, loyally upheld, is vital, mere command to do it in this or that way, exclusive of all other ideas on the point, will never succeed. Autocracy (with the lid on) may succeed elsewhere—never in church. One is reminded of the remark of a sixth-form boy to his wisely companionable headmaster at table one day : "Head, you are eating too fast !" "Oh, thank you, my boy." Such working humility among efficient leaders and encouragement of respectful candour at practice would banish its devastating opposite of covert discussion of shortcomings out of earshot of the supposed shortcomer. This frankness is within the reach of all.

It has already been pointed out that among choral

bodies the church choir is *sui generis*, and the term necessarily applies also to its discipline and leadership. The
well-disciplined choir is known less by its singing of
extended works (in which field it has much in common
with a choral society) than by its ability to overcome
the difficulties that are peculiar to its constitution and
work. These are worth a little discussion from a practical point of view.

As is shown in Chapter V., the singers work under
very different conditions from those that govern any
other performing body of musicians. Much of the
activity—often the largest part of it, indeed—is inevitably concerned with routine. Week in, week out,
year after year, the same small but vitally important
things have to be said or sung, the same physical acts
of devotion and deportment carried out. It is fatally
easy for the routine to become "mere," and the acts
casual and slovenly. Too often the responses, Amens,
and other details are half-hearted and flabby ; the walk
degenerates into a slouch, the kneeling into a crouch.
These faults are hard to cure because the matters in
which they occur lend themselves less well to practice
than do the more substantial and attractive parts of
the service. The perfect response, monotone, and
Amen may be achieved with ease in the practice room :
the difficulty lies in transplanting this perfection into
the choir-stalls. The perfect detail in any affair of
routine results, not from the fitful crusade, but from the
careful habit. The crusade may be indispensable, but as
it is usually the result of some weeks of slackness, it
ought to be regarded as a costly remedy, and its need

avoided by constant watchfulness on the part of the choirmaster. The parson, too, has his responsibility here : a slovenly response to a slovenly versicle is far more a matter of cause and effect than is usually realized. Indeed, the degree to which a choir is sub-consciously affected by the reading, intoning, and general conduct of the service by the officiant is a factor that, so far as our observation goes, is rarely considered.

We suggest that the simplest and most effective way of dealing with the *minutiæ* of a choir's work—responses, Amens, walking in procession, standing, and kneeling— is to regard them together as a matter of demeanour or deportment, and to deal with them systematically. For the singing of a plain Amen or response depends less on musical ability than on attention, just as seemliness in physical attitude and processional walking is a detail of good conduct, not a feat of athleticism : both are, in short, merely good choir manners.

It will generally be found that a choir will respond readily to an appeal based on this ground. Nobody likes to be accounted ill-mannered, and it ought not to be hard to show that the code for the sanctuary, like that for every kind of social meeting-place, is based on thoughtfulness and consideration, plus that highest kind of good manners known simply as reverence.

Still, some kind of practice may be necessary, and it is a good plan to set apart a few minutes of one rehearsal per month or so for the overhauling of responses and Amens; and, as the casual singing of responses is sometimes due to the use of one set only, it is advisable to ring the changes on two or three.* So far as processional walking is concerned, an occasional rehearsal is necessary ; and if such a useful official as a *ceremoniarius* is available, the choir should be handed over to him for the occasion. In default, the parson should at least be at hand, if only in order to help the choir to realize that the need for care and thoughtfulness on their part does not end (though it may begin) with the music.

It may be useful to consider a few further practical points. Slovenliness in standing and kneeling is often the result of inconveniently planned seats and desks. Such furniture is usually an antique fixture, often more pleasing to the eye of the visitor than to the anatomy of the user. A good deal may be done in such cases by the provision of hassocks or kneeling-racks of a convenient height ; and desks may often be made more practicable without serious damage to their appearance. In furnishing a new church, or in replacing old choir-stalls by new, among the first points that ought to be considered are practicability and convenience. Let the various designs and measurements be tested in the only satisfactory way, *i.e.* by experimental use of the boys and men, kneeling, sitting, and standing ; the height of the desk ought to be such that prayer-books can be used kneeling and music-books standing, *without handling*.

* Choirs that are accustomed to unaccompanied singing of fairly difficult five-part polyphony, should consider the collection of "Responses by Tudor Composers," recently issued by the Church Music Society, edited by Sir Ivor Atkins and Dr. E. H. Fellowes (Oxford University Press, 1s. 6d.).

Holding a heavyish volume during a long stretch of singing is tiring for the singers and very bad for the book; indeed, the lifetime of all the choir music (especially single copies of anthems and services) is more than doubled if it can live on the desk instead of in the hands—sometimes hot and careless—of the singers. (This latter point applies also to the furnishing of the practice room.)

As to walking, whether it be merely a progress from vestry to choir stalls, or a liturgical procession, mere commonsense will rule out the swinging arms, the stride, and the roll. A choir should need only an occasional reminder that (1) steps should be short; (2) the feet should be placed almost as if walking a plank (this automatically cures a tendency to sway from side to side); (3) when no books are carried the arms should hang easily with no more than a suspicion of a swing (some choirmasters favour folded arms, but two things are to be said against this: the pose is not natural, and when it happens to be combined with a roll, the result is doubly unfortunate); (4) the procession should suggest walking in files rather than in pairs; the width between files should be a couple of yards or so (rather less than more) if the dimensions of the passage-way allow; and the walkers should follow each other at about an arm's length. (The measurement should not be guesswork: it should be ascertained at an occasional rehearsal by the simple process of each member placing his hands on the shoulders of the member in front: the space will soon be subconsciously maintained.) We return to that word "natural": it is not

8

natural for boys to walk with downcast eyes and hands clasped as if in prayer : the method may suit the illustrated catalogues of church furnishers in which it so often figures, but it doesn't belong to real life. Finally, the choir (*and* the clergy) should look neither to the right nor to the left ; a roving eye and a distracted mind go together. Good choir-walking is a substantial addition to the dignity of a service : straggling, jostling, staring, and arm-swinging are bad manners, made worse when displayed by the very people whose duty and privilege it is to set the standard.

CHAPTER VII

THE PART OF THE CLERGY

THE musical responsibilities of the parson are three-fold : (*a*) To the art itself, (*b*) to the organist and choir, and (*c*) to the congregation. As to (*a*) : there can be no fitly sung liturgy without a musically competent officiant. The term "musically competent" is not exacting, for it demands no more than ability to take a note, and to use the singing voice in tune, rhythmically, and with reasonably good tone in the preces at Mattins and Evensong ; in monotoning the Collects ; and in singing the *Sursum Corda* and Prefaces and the Creed and Gloria intonations at the choral celebration of Holy Communion. These simple requirements can be easily met by all but the tiny minority who are tone-deaf. If those who are not so afflicted are content to remain incompetent, they are setting a poor example to the organist and choir, who co-operate with them in these portions of the service, and who therefore have a right to expect the necessary degree of accuracy. The Report of the Archbishop's Committee is unequivocal on this point. The following is from the section headed "The Parson" :

> ". . . when he cannot sing the officiant's part accurately, it is better that he should not attempt it, and that in that case the singing of responses should be dropped. This need not prevent the

singing of the *Sanctus*, though that, properly speaking, is continuous with the versicles and preface. These the celebrant must sing at the pitch corresponding with the *Sanctus*, or not at all. But other versicles and responses can be sung at any pitch which may suit him, inasmuch as they link on to nothing but the reciting note of the prayer following them : and there is no difficulty in the singers taking their pitch from him provided they sing in unison. Similarly the "Amens" should not be sung unless the prayer has been said upon a fixed note."

As the necessary type of musical training is now being added to the curriculum in an increasing proportion of Theological Colleges, such an anomaly as a sung office being spoilt by the officiant should soon cease to be (as it is now) of frequent occurrence.

The requirements discussed above constitute the minimum of what may be required musically of the parson. A great deal more is often asked of him, however, and it is in view of such contingencies that the Report emphasizes the need in Theological Colleges for a musical training, simple indeed, yet far beyond the preces and monotone stage. The Report says :

"We feel constrained to urge that it is essential. The clergy in every parish in the country now have to take a leading part in services that in some degree are musical ; in many places—numerically, indeed, in most—they must direct them, unless some more competent musician can be found or paid for. Often it is on the parson, or perhaps on his wife, that the duty falls of supervising at least, if not actually directing, the music.

"The question therefore arises as to the proportion of educated men who are incapable of music. It has been said that tone-deafness is as rare as colour-blindness ; and, if this is so, it is clear that we are wrong if either in Church or State we treat music as an educational luxury for the few."

(b) The incumbent's position in regard to the organist is a frequent cause of misunderstanding on both sides. The ultimate responsibility for the music of a parish church rests with the incumbent, who "has the right of directing the service, e.g., when the organ shall and shall not play, and when the children shall and shall not chant, though the organist is paid and the children managed by the churchwardens."* "Organists have no legal status, and no ecclesiastical position as such."† Cripps's "Law Relating to Church and Clergy" is more explicit, and shows in what other ways the organist is, legally, of no account :

"As the minister is to direct at his discretion what parts of the service are to be sung, and to exercise a general superintendence in such matters, it follows that he may direct by whom the singing and chanting are to be principally performed, whether it be instrumental or vocal, and, in fact, make any new orders or regulations relating thereto as he may think fit, but subject to the general controlling power of the ordinary, who is the proper person to consider complaints. The

* Blunt and Phillimore, "The Book of Church Law" (quoted in Archbishop's Report).
† *Ibid.*

appointment or dismissal of singers or instrumental performers in the church rests entirely with the minister, who might dismiss them individually or as a body, appoint a different method, or prohibit singing altogether, if he thought proper, subject, however, as we have already observed."

This undignified position of an important official (especially in regard to insecurity of tenure) is utterly opposed to common-sense and the good of the church. "The music-director's position should be made secure against arbitrary dismissal or capricious action, and an appeal should lie to the Bishop."* The formation of parochial councils has eased the organist's situation somewhat, inasmuch as the incumbent is far less likely to take any kind of strong action without the knowledge or consent of the congregation's representatives: but legally the position remains as stated in the above quotation.

Many causes of friction would be removed by the formation of a Church Music Committee consisting of the clergy, the organist and choirmaster, the church-wardens, and a group of representative men and women of the congregation. In addition to the help it could give in the settlement of differences by discussion, such a committee might well play a useful part in assisting the development of the organist's plans in regard to congregational singing, the provision of books for choir and people, the supply of recruits for the choir, etc.

Relations between parson and organist have improved

* Archbishop's Report.

during recent years, partly because organists generally are not only better qualified musically, but also wider in their interests and therefore more companionable. The Organists' Associations have done much good work in this respect, by periodically bringing together the organists of a district for social meetings, rambles, lectures, and discussions (*not* always on music, wisely), and so forth; and the frequent co-operation of the clergy in the Association's activities is another helpful factor. On their side the clergy are realizing the wisdom of appointing as their musical director a thoroughly competent man, and then leaving him to do the work.

The attitude that should *not* be taken is implicit in the question an ordinand asked a cathedral organist who had been lecturing at a Theological College: "To what extent shall I be able to interfere with my organist?" We do not know the organist's reply, but it might have been on these lines: "The question is apt, and shows a praiseworthy desire to avoid an unduly oppressive attitude towards subordinates. You will be able to interfere, legally, far more than you probably imagine. Thus, as the custody of the organ is yours, you may forbid its use at any time, ensuring obedience by locking it and losing the key. If the organist uses it for teaching purposes, it must be with your consent. As to wedding and other fees: professional custom (based on common-sense and courtesy) rules that they are payable to the organist, even though the bride's second cousin plays at the ceremony. You may, however, override mere professional custom, and so enable a couple to begin their married life by economizing on the commodity that in England is a popular means of retrenchment, *i.e.*, music. You will find it easy to get rid of an organist who doesn't suit you ; he is, in fact, easier to sack than the sexton. This is hard on the organist, whose income usually depends less on his church salary than on the teaching connection that he has laboriously built up. If you force him to change his post he will usually have to begin all over again. You should therefore think at least twice before dismissing him. It may interest you to know that this right of arbitrary dismissal of the organist by the parson was so frequently exercised in the past, and led to so much hardship, that as recently as 1917 the matter was brought to the notice of the Archbishop of Canterbury by a deputation from the Royal College of Organists. To proceed : You may at any time alter the entire musical character of the services, introducing plainsong, or a new hymnal, or florid settings, without consulting anybody ; the choir, like the organist, is at your complete disposal, and you may decide to do without them whenever it pleases you. It seems incredible that all this power is vested in one who may be entirely unmusical, but there it is. In fine, all these things are lawful for you ; but . . ."

Does this sound bitter ? If so, the bitterness is not towards the clergy, who nowadays—to their honour be it said—rarely take advantage of their legal position. The imaginary reply to the actual ordinand is a summary of the incumbent's rights and the organists' wrongs ; and it expresses the feeling of organists concerning conditions of employment that dishonour both the church and the art and profession of music.

Happily, there is an increasing amount of virtue in that "but" : all the available evidence shows that the relations between clergy and organist are better than they have ever been. Occasional disputes are exploited by the cheaper press, for the good reason that they make better "copy" than the harmony that now generally reigns : to most parsons their organist is a "good fellow," to most organists their vicar is "one of the best." And it is a happy augury that this greatly improved state of things coincides with the widespread awakening of interest in church music.

(c) The parson's musical responsibility to his congregation is to a considerable extent bound up with his relationship to organist and choir. Experience shows that the majority of a congregation can be persuaded to agree to considerable changes in the musical arrangements if the matter is handled tactfully. For example, the introduction of a new hymnal may split a congregation beyond reunion if the change is made without due preparation and discussion. A general meeting of officials, choir, and people is usually the best opening move ; and if the meeting can be addressed by the organist (who should back up his remarks on the musical advantages of the proposed change by a few choice examples sung by the choir) so much the better. The Parochial Council or the Church Music Committee should then go into the matter thoroughly, after a few weeks' personal examination of copies ; and, the new book having been introduced, the utmost tact should be used in the choice of tunes until it has become established. New tunes should not be "shot at" the people, but their successful introduction ensured by congregational practices. This is an instance of the kind of episode that, well handled, unites parson, organist, choir, and congregation. The method described is not mere theory : it was adopted at a London church within a few months of the publication of the "English Hymnal." (In an adjacent parish it happened that the book was introduced in the inconsiderate way with disastrous results.)

In all the musical matters of a parish church the need is for co-operation between parson, organist, and people, even in regard to apparently unimportant details. This must not, however, be allowed to derogate from the position and authority of either parson or organist. The parson has the last word on the liturgical side ; and the organist (we assume one duly qualified) should be the ultimate authority on the music—despite the legal ruling quoted at the beginning of the chapter. Differences there must be, and in a surprisingly large number of instances they will be the result, not of slackness on either side, but of keenness. Regret need not be wasted on such crises : they serve a purpose. Met as they should be met by colleagues in the service of the Church, their solution will prove, like "the falling out of faithful friends," to be yet one more bond of union.

CHAPTER VIII

SOLOS AND SOLOISTS

A GLANCE at the solo anthems of the Restoration period will show that one of the most recurrent and insidiously besetting sins of music as the voice of worship is found in the solo performance in church. And yet what is to be done? What finer sermon in the world, at the fitting moment, than Handel's "He was despised"? Even the composer himself was, we are told, melted to tears by its performance. Who that has ever heard the solo in that old anthem of Wise's, "The ways of Zion," can forget the experience? A little play upon the words may here help to clear the point and indicate its solution. Music can be the voice of worship; but, when a single voice carries the whole burden, it may degenerate into the worship of voice. This is the crux.

So great is the danger that it needs a short chapter to itself, and (to our regret) the chapter must begin in the style of a friendly homily to those gifted with a fine voice. If a parson went home after preaching, praying or reading, and said to his wife: "Wasn't I in fine voice?" one hopes she might reply, "What about the Gospel?" But if a singer does the same, the remark seems to need little or no correction. Yet it is certain that soloists who think of their own powers while singing will induce a subtle diversion from the main issue among the worshippers; personal admirations or dislikes will set in; and ultimately comes the degeneration spoken of above.

It is far from our intention to disparage a fine voice and its utmost cultivation. We desire only to stimulate serviceable reflection among soloists themselves, and those who control church music; for, even when the singer is above reproach and wholly self-effacing without effort, as, happily, the average solo boy is, congregations still have a way of going from church thinking rather of the singer than of the song.

There seems one paramount suggestion to make, apart from recommending the fullest development of choral songs as being naturally more impersonal and to the point in church than solo songs. The suggestion is mainly offered to the singer, and it is this: Consider every solo note sung in the course of a service as sung *on behalf of the whole choir*; that is, form the habit of feeling the burden of the musical thought of the *many* upon the mind of *one*, that one happening for the moment to be yourself. This can scarcely fail to release you from self-consciousness, which is at all times a singer's natural bugbear, and, of course, a deadly enemy to worship. It can scarcely fail to give you new zest and certainly new responsibility—yes, and responsiveness too. Your power to put every ounce of life and thought and voice and judgment into the beauty of the sung words will steadily increase with the formation of such a habit. Incidentally it will tend wholesomely to unify the solo and choral parts of any given anthem, and tend towards the attainment of that ideal state of worship-music wherein the listener will scarcely be aware whether the medium is a voice or an instrument, or one voice or many.*

Some practical aspects of the question may now be discussed. There are clergy and choirmasters who, considering only the undesirable possibilities of solo-ism touched on above, object to any form of solo sing-ing. Undoubtedly there is a risk of both vanity and jealousy ; but is the avoidance of the risk worth the cost of one of the most natural and effective means of obtaining variety and contrast ? On moral and musical grounds alike it is surely better to develop to the ut-most the musical potentialities of the choir, in the in-dividual and the section no less than in the mass, and to be prompt with the word in season when the soloists tend to show vanity and the non-soloists jealousy.

The degree of risk will, of course, depend largely on whether the choir is composed of keen church members who regard their work as a duty and privilege, or of ambitious singers to whom the church choir presents an attractive weekly public platform. The keen church members are not immune from vanity and jealousy ; but their presence in the choir is due to a sense of duty and responsibility that makes it possible for the choir-master or parson to appeal to them on grounds that mean little or nothing to singers whose qualifications are purely vocal. It cannot be too tenaciously remem-bered that the best generator of the spirit of co-opera-

* Santley's maxim, " Sing mentally during the rests," may be recalled in this connection, as the ideal for all choirs when one of their number is singing alone.

tion in the church choir is always the spirit of worship itself, the expression of which is the choir's *raison d'être*. The point has been fully discussed in Chapter V.; it is referred to here because it crops up in regard to the solo question, as it will crop up in many other connections. Experience will show that there is hardly any problem in the morale and discipline of the adult section of a choir that is not readily solved if one of the qualifications for membership of the choir is membership of the church. A less stringent method of recruitment may produce numbers ; it will certainly be popular; and by its inclusiveness it is likely to lead to considerable musical results. But the success will be bought at a price, and the music sung may be the voice of something other than worship. For when a choir is allowed to develop into an undenominational concert party the congregation is likely to degenerate into an admission-free audience.

We have said that the various forms of solo singing are natural and effective means of obtaining variety and contrast. It is unfortunate that the term "solo" has been reduced to its narrowest meaning, literally correct though that meaning may be. Much of the dislike of the mere word "solo" in connection with parish church music is due to this fact. Now, the genuine soloist is born rather than made: to the qualities produced by training must be added others that no amount of training can give, although it may help in their development, *i.e.* imagination, individuality and the faculty of simultaneously generating and controlling the touch of incandescence—we had almost said excitement—that differentiates a moving interpretation from a mere delivery of the text. Nor is the born soloist distinguished by these attributes alone. Voice counts, too, but here the important factors are not of the usual vocal type. You may hear a choirmaster say of a boy or man, "Yes : a capital voice for chorus work, but not a solo voice." In other words it has power and range, but lacks character, appeal, colour—qualities that can, in fact, reveal themselves to the full only when the voice possessing them is heard alone. The average church choir may be without a genuine soloist for a long spell ; or it may enjoy a vintage period with several. Refusal to make use of such a gift on the ground that the singer may become vain, or his colleagues jealous, is waste of a precious gift—a waste that cannot be justified. To bury one's own talent is bad ; to bury that of others is surely worse.

Hardly less to be deprecated is the irresponsible undertaking of solos by singers lacking the real solo voice and temperament, the more so as there is an admirable quasi-solo effect available in every choir fairly strong in numbers. This substitute—too little employed, so far as our observation goes—may be described by the apparently contradictory term "solo-ensemble." A passage for treble solo sounds far better when sung by a dozen quite ordinary voices that have been unified than it does when treated as a solo, unless the soloist be first rate. Individually, not one of the dozen may be capable of singing alone even a verse of a simple hymn ; collectively, they are rarely less than pleasing ; at their best they are transformed into a choral medium of extraordinary appeal. Moreover, the preparation of a solo-ensemble number is one of the best forms of training. The music being purely melodic, and lightly accompanied, demands an unusually high degree of unity in tone and precision in utterance : defects that might pass in part-singing are mercilessly exposed in a solo-ensemble. On all grounds, therefore, this use of boys' voices is to be encouraged. The music suitable for the purpose varies so widely in character and degree of difficulty that there is something for boys of every degree of attainment, from an occasional verse of a hymn or psalm up to brilliant oratorio songs such as "Let the bright seraphim," or some expressive aria of Bach. And, we repeat, the excellence achieved in any one of them, from the simplest to the most elaborate, is reflected in the singers' work in general.

There is much to be said for a similar treatment of tenor and bass solos. Modern composers, indeed, seem to be ahead of choirmasters in their realization of this, for they frequently give such optional directions as "tenor solo (or all the tenors)." A familiar example of the fine effect of a men's-voice solo-ensemble is the section "Being born again" in S. S. Wesley's "Blessed be the God and Father." Passages of a quiet melodic character for all the tenors or basses of a choir, or for tenors and basses together, ought to be not less effective than the dramatic quasi-recitative in Wesley's anthem. A few merely ordinary voices, of poor effect heard singly, will together produce a composite result that in tone, colour, and vitality far exceeds what would be expected from the constituents. For it is a fact—

well established, but too little regarded among choral trainers—that the defects of individuals cancel one another in the mass. Thus it is often remarked (with surprise) that a crowd of untrained and mostly indifferent voices heard together do not sound like (say) a hundred indifferent voices, but like a large good one of a new and curiously moving—even thrilling—sort. And this is true of even a small well-directed force of men or boys : the sum is immeasurably superior to the parts.

The most important solo-ensemble, however, is the quartet. Here, again, it will be found that four quite ordinary voices can, by diligent practice, develop into a highly artistic unit. Indeed, the best results are not usually obtained from solo voices. A proof of this unexpected fact is to be heard at a performance of "Elijah," where the quartet is usually better sung by four members of the chorus than by the soloists. For the very qualities that distinguish born soloists—individuality, temperament, and marked tonal characteristics—are apt to make them unsatisfactory in ensemble. The best quartets are often the result of mere competence plus co-operation.

The musical possibilities of a good quartet—the team within the team—are almost inexhaustible. They may be given any quiet section of an anthem or " setting," a fauxbourdon to a verse of a hymn or psalm (the throwing into relief of an occasional verse of a psalm, by this and other means discussed in Chapter X., is a device rarely used: even a single verse so treated can vitalize a whole psalm) ; they provide one of the

9

most natural of musical effects when singing antiphonally with the remainder of the choir; and, not least,
they make possible a neglected but beautiful and traditional method of harmonizing portions of the liturgical
chant sung by the congregation and led by the rest of
the choir. At present such harmonizing is almost confined to the organ.

Choirs strong in numbers and of good average
quality should possess both decani and cantoris quartets, and the two combined give yet another team within the team—a semi-chorus, thus opening up further
possibilities in variety, and especially in antiphony;
and where resources are ample the personnel of the
quartets may be changed from time to time in order
that the interest might be spread and the benefit of the
experience and training extended to as many members
as possible. Something analogous to the rota system
of cathedral choirs might be adopted: just as the
cathedral choir has its decani and cantoris "verse"
weeks, the large church choir should have its decani
and cantoris quartet and semi-chorus or "verse"
months. Let no choirmaster think this is over-elabora-
tion: most of the weaknesses of parish church music
are due to a lack of system. There is far too much of
the characteristic English go-as-you-please, hand-to-
mouth method, and far too little planning; and one of
the worst results of this absence of policy is the casual
attendance in voluntary choirs. Some form of rota, by
detailing a proportion of the members for regular
special duty, develops a sense of responsibility. It may
be argued that members of the quartet might be

irregular in attendance when not on special duty. The answer is two-fold : such members are likely to be irregular under any circumstances ; and regular attendance during periods of obligation should surely do much to develop the right habit. We are convinced, in fact, that the policy of the team-within-the-team would ultimately justify itself no less on disciplinary than on musical grounds. The theory that all the members are equally important all the time is attractive, but in practice it is apt to end in unanimous *un*importance.

There remain the choirs unable to raise even a quartet : what is left for them in the way of quasi-solo ? They have the answer in the almost universal method of antiphonal chanting. The decani and cantoris arrangement should be applied to other parts of the service. Hymns present an obvious field. It might well be a regular practice for all hymns containing more than three verses to be sung by alternate sides, excepting the first and last, which should be always full—the first in order to ensure a good lead for the congregation, the last because the principles of musical performance demand a climax at that point (a climax not necessarily of power ; quiet unanimity can be even more impressive). The "full" treatment should also be applied to any verse midway that calls for it. Confusion as to the allotment of verses can be avoided by the simple expedient of adopting the plan used in chanting the psalms : the sides automatically take even or odd verses. Half-hearted singing of hymns—especially long ones—results mainly from fatigue and lack of interest and variety. After having sung the Mattins canticles and psalms, a choir (especially one with imperfect methods of voice production) is apt to peter out, show signs of strain, or to rest in spasms during long hymns. It is surely better that the resting should be done by sides, with a purpose. Moreover (since even when decani and cantoris are well-balanced and well-trained, there is pretty sure to be some slight difference in vocal colour), the antiphony provides welcome contrast as well as ensuring a greater degree of diligence than is usually achieved when everybody is optimistically expected to sing everything. A further method of obtaining variety and ensuring brief periods of rest is the giving of occasional verses to boys and men in alternation. The question of compass must, of course, be considered: the tune must not be so low as to be ineffective for trebles, or so high as to be a strain for the men. So far as the latter are concerned, it should be remembered that an occasional high note matters far less than the general "lie" of the tune—its *tessitura*, to use the technical term. (In Chapter IX. more is said concerning the varied treatment of hymns.)

As with psalms and hymns, so with anthems and settings of the canticles. In any but the very shortest examples opportunity should be found for the antiphony of decani and cantoris—not so much for the resting of the voices as for the provision of variety and the development of responsibility and confidence; for there are obvious psychological reasons why anthems may be far less tiring than psalms and hymns.

We have tried to show that in all but the smallest and least well-equipped of choirs there are possibilities of solo and quasi-solo utterance waiting to be developed. A reader asks, "Isn't this over-organization?" Let the answer be in the form of further questions : Is it more than (or even as much as) any enterprising choral society or orchestra would find advisable ? Has any church choir been wrecked through too much planning and looking ahead ? Hasn't many a choir stagnated through lack of it ? And can any system that develops a choir's possibilities, both individual and corporate, be other than good ? The musical gains are obvious ; and, given wise direction, nothing but good (and a great deal of it) can result on the social and disciplinary side. We cannot believe that a properly-constituted Church choir would be rent by jealousy and dissension because some of its members are given the opportunity of using their gifts to the full in the service of the church. It is surely not too much to expect of a singing team the reasonableness of a cricket team, which plays some members specially for their bowling and some for their batting (the soloists, so to speak), others for their fielding and general proficiency (the purely chorus members), and even includes a few others less for what they are than for what they promise to become with practice (the probationers). Is a cricket team in danger of breaking up because the captain consistently arranges the order of batting in accordance with the players' ability, or opens the attack with his best bowlers ?

CHAPTER IX

CONGREGATIONAL SINGING

CONGREGATIONAL singing, the world over, is probably most associated with hymn singing, and both the beauties and the defects of our hymn-tunes are perhaps accounted for by this fact. When a mass of worshippers sing together, not only is an agreed metre or measure of lines something between a convenience and a necessity, but an agreed pattern or measure of related longs and shorts is also a most natural and quickly acceptable unifier of massed utterance. Think first of the common-metre pattern as we know it today: its reliable alternative of seven syllables with six are made to meet the needs of the largest number of the simplest people, and, incidentally, it gives a very convenient half-way house (at the end of the second line) for breathing, and for rallying, too. But all too soon it can become dead-alive, by reason of the uniformity of note-value prescribed to be helpful. Think next of the simple agreed phrase-patterns of long and short such as the familiar

or Monk's "Eventide." It will easily be seen how that life, interest and unifying power would all be lessened the moment these patterns are ironed out into metres of equal notes :

What Dr. Geoffrey Shaw neatly calls the "minimity" of our congregational singing has accounted for much, both of its great quality and sad defects in past years. It is glorious to hear the vitalized congregational minim in the merely metrical 8 6 (C.M.) ploughing along, gathering momentum, for ever uniform, for ever free—serving as the inspired stride of such a great hymnal utterance as, *e.g.* :

God moves in a mys-ter-ious way His won-ders to   per-form.

But it is depressing to watch the effect of this very thing in decay ; listless lazy minims begin to succeed each other in dreary monotony for perhaps eight times twenty-eight dead notes, with equally deadening pauses every eighth, fourteenth, twenty-second and twenty-eighth notes. Children may be seen looking about them listlessly as their grown-ups go on their minim-izing way. Men of ideas stand bored. Young people remain outside the church, letting distance and fading respect supply what little dying enchantment this thing can retain.

The preservation of the real thing and the removal

of its abuse, both of them, can be secured only by a contagion of enthusiasm. It is no cure of this particular minimity to requisition lilting folk-songs. On the other hand, to oppose the present post-English Hymnal vogue for these is to forget the inherent oneness of a folk love-song (at its best) with a folk Christian-song. Lilt is a heavenly attribute whether in the one or the other. And here we are back at the patterned hymn-tunes, the second kind of congregational tune mentioned above. The extreme instance is to be found in the tune "Helmsley," which proved to be closely akin to a popular hornpipe "as danced by Miss Catley at Sadler's Wells," and yet became associated for a century or more with what is perhaps the most solemn of Advent hymns. Even this coincidence need not drive us to an extreme dislike of metrical pattern in hymn-tunes. The hymnal of the future will probably contain in equal abundance both metrical tunes of *unvaried* note-values and those of fittingly *varied* note-values. The Old Hundredth will survive, we hope, in both variants :

and

If choice were offered, we should, without hesitation, choose the first for public school use. With the semibreve as unit, it has interest, thrust, animation; and boys would be well served by all these in both hymn and tune. For 5,000 people singing in the Albert Hall on some significant moving national occasion, it might well be that the minims would refuse to be short enough to make the semibreves bearable. So the majestic stride already referred to would assert itself, and—away with pattern as an inadequate unserviceable attribute, at such a moment, with such a concourse.

In Chapter XI. the choice of tunes is discussed from its present-day practical and (it may be added) often embarrassing angle. Here we desire to centre our readers' thoughts upon the necessity for the vital acceptance of *both* orders of congregational hymn-melody, and to point out that failure in either will be best averted if both the unpatterned and the patterned line or phrase—which are the units of congregational song—be accepted and both more diligently vitalized, and congregations given opportunity for and help into their natural *stride* in both kinds. It is painful to hear adult Christians singing childish, snippety rhythmic patterns, slowly, to hymns of adult character. When a tune gathers momentum while it is sung, verse by verse, till the last verse sounds "full-out" and thrilling, this splendid result is usually due to the happy discovery of the right tune for the congregation that so sings it. It is the business not only of the editors of every hymnal but of every parson and choirmaster to try patiently to discover and use such tunes. This elementary matter of *momentum* is too often ignored. For example, an organist will play a tune over in a lifeless, rhythmless way, or at an obviously unsuitable pace ; even if he plays at the right swing for the congregation, the parson will perhaps arrest the momentum and stop the whole proceeding to read out the first verse ; the congregation will then struggle to its feet ; and the hymn will finally make a start—of the kind that may be expected after such preliminaries.

Hymn singing is the largest musical part for the congregation. It may not be, however, their chief part in the ideal service. One can, indeed, imagine that the perfect unity of choir and congregation for a single moment in one fervent Amen may be a more memorable and significant part of any good service than any other musical moment in it. And it is good to realize that by far the most hopeful sign on the church-music horizon in England today seems to lie in the direction prefigured by Robert Bridges in all he said and tried to do for chanting our language in its most natural way. Chanting is fully dealt with in its own chapter later. But of precisely the same order of natural singing for multitudes together are the Amens, responses and refrains. When these are at their fervent best, and congregations are given a melody that is right for its purpose in pace, pitch, speed, rhythm, speech-inflection, and always of fitting loudness and softness, we are likely to realize hopes already raised.

It may now be useful to turn from general considerations to the present position and the immediate opportunities that are likely to offer for advancement along sound lines, be it by ever so small a step at the moment. Although it is a first need that Amens, responses, petitions and refrains be kept so simple as to be well within the powers of the people, this general need and policy must not rule out the occasional and timely elaboration of Amens that have special significance, in which only the choir and experienced musical worshipper can take part. For when devotion grows profound, devout musicians incline to enrich the expression and tax or outstrip congregational ability by adding notes in various ways that involve both melodic and harmonic elaboration. This is seen in the Dresden Amen, and in Stainer's well-known and often impertinently derided sevenfold example;* and it is easy to see how an Amen which arises spontaneously out of heart-felt utterance, designed to give worshippers ampler endorsement of their own prayer, begins also, by the very same natural process, to grow into a form too ornate for use. This crossing of the line between that which is and is not congregational is likely to be in constant need of watching and ordering rightly as between congregation and choir. For example, it should not rule out the use, on special occasions, and by skilled choirs, of the beautiful responses by Byrd, Morley, and other early composers. The greater church festivals may well be marked in this way ; and such occasional change from the usual settings is incidentally a preventive of the staleness that is apt to result from unbroken repetition of the

* The mere mention of Stainer's sevenfold Amen is sufficient to raise a smile among " superior " church musicians who tolerate —and even advocate—a good deal of music that is no better in quality, though it may be of more distinguished origin. Objectors ought to state frankly whether their dislike is due to its sevenfold character or to the name of its composer. The first is a reasonable ground of objection ; the second is not.

simpler musical details of a service. The so-called
Festival Responses of Tallis should be reserved for such
special use. As at present used, they are uncongrega-
tional. In theory the people should sing the simple
plainsong inflections that form the core of Tallis's
setting; but as these inflections are not very easily
traceable throughout, it is not surprising that the people
either remain silent, or (what is sometimes worse) try
to sing the treble part, which only sopranos and tenors
can manage comfortably. Hence the advisability of
adopting, for normal use, such simple responses as the
set issued by the Church Music Society, or a good
edition (that is, one with appropriately strong and
simple harmonies) of the responses known as Tallis's
Ferial, or of those in the "Manual of Plainsong"
(Novello, 1d.). They should be sung unaccompanied
if possible, and the method should clearly be that of
good chanting. Congregational singing of such parts
of the Liturgy can be surprisingly impressive; and a
hearty co-operation of choir and people in the opening
responses is usually followed by good congregational
singing during the remainder of the service. On the
other hand, there are few more depressing experiences
than to find the opening invocation, "O Lord, open
Thou our lips," followed by stubborn silence in the
nave.

Good congregational singing of the psalms is an
ideal at present but rarely attained. The canticles and
a few of the more frequently used psalms are manage-
able by the people, because the pointing becomes
memorized; but, in general, congregational chanting

demands congregational psalters and practices. We have known excellent results from the provision of a few dozen copies of the pointed psalter provided, like hymn-books, for the people's use ; indeed, the interest roused has been so great that many members have bought copies for themselves. At the church we have in mind, a monthly congregational practice was the rule, and the psalms for the ensuing Evensong were practised. Concerning the methods of holding a congregational practice, more will be said later. Here we wish to endorse and emphasize the view that congregational singing will never even approach its best until a start is made on the principle that the fundamental principles of choralism should be aimed at in the nave no less than in the choir. Attack, unanimity, vital tone and rhythm : these call for no degree of skill beyond that attainable by any normally intelligent crowd of adults. The congregation, though a large body, ought not to need time to "get under way" : their start ought to be as alert as that of the choir; they ought to move as firmly, and to show the same feeling for rise and fall and climax. It is not too much to say that in these primary matters the singers in the nave ought to be as good as those in the choir, the main difference between the two bodies being that the latter are called on to add to those fundamentals certain other qualities demanded by the more difficult music assigned to them. The singing congregation should, in fact, regard itself as an extension of the choir from the chancel to the nave, just as the choir is a portion of the congregation promoted from the nave to the chancel in order to carry out certain duties for which it is qualified and prepared.

To mention this distinction between the two bodies is to indicate the cause of frequent failure in congregational singing. A glance at plainsong shows that the early Church provided for both skilled and unskilled singers. Probably the impetus to congregational singing given by the publication of "Hymns Ancient and Modern" did some damage by encouraging people to join in such anthems (or portions of them) as were familiar. Be that as it may, the line of demarcation has become absurdly obscured, and, despite the improved state of congregational singing, there are still too many churches where the people are either entirely silent or not silent enough. At first sight the latter appears to be the lesser evil; but where everybody tries to sing everything, nobody sings anything really well. Is half-hearted singing better than none at all? We doubt it. Plainly the need is for frank facing of facts, followed by organization. It is unfortunate that so many clergy shirk the simple task of conferring with their organist and then making the result known either in the parish magazine or by a few words during the service.

In churches where there is a capable choir it is insufficient to tell the people that their hearty co-operation is desired: this vagueness often leads to unhappy results, for there will always be a few disposed to rush in and co-operate heartily at the wrong moment. The principle should be clearly laid down that there are parts of the service for the choir alone, and for choir and people combined ; later may come the further sub-division of choir alone, choir and people together, and people alone. Even this does not exhaust the easy possibilities of variety and contrast—not merely for their own sake, but because of the part those qualities play in vitalizing a service. A book rich in historical interest, "Congregational Hymn-Singing in England," by Dr. W. T. Whitley, has recently been published by Messrs. Dent. Its final chapter, by Dr. Eric Thiman, entitled "Recent Thought and Tendency in Congregational Singing," deals so fully and common-sensibly with the topic under discussion that we refer the reader to it. A passage on this matter of organization, however, ought to be quoted here. After discussing faux-bourdons and descants as a means of variety, Dr. Thiman adds :

"There is one further variety of congregational unison singing which is not explored as much as it might be ; for not only is it easy of performance, needing no special parts or elaborate preparation, but it is in addition probably as old as religion itself ; and it is strange that ministers and organists, knowing something of the method of singing the psalms employed in the temple at Jerusalem in pre-Christian times, do not make more use of the practice and possibilities of antiphonal singing. One sometimes hears hymns thus treated, with verses taken alternately by women's and by men's voices, to a tune such as *O Filii et Filiæ* or *Veni Emmanuel*, which does not permit of harmony singing ; and undeniably effective all will admit it to be, especially when the antiphonal verses are alternated with verses sung "full." But it is not generally realized that a most effective extension of this idea might be arranged by dividing the congregation up into, for instance, north gallery, south gallery, and transept, for succeeding verses, the whole congregation to take the first and last. Few organists will have heard this done, and many will probably have no conception of how thrilling the "full" verses become when contrasted with the "sectional" ones. So simple is the idea that one can only marvel that it has not been tried to any extent; and as for the initial arrangements, it would only be necessary for the minister when announcing the hymn to indicate the allocation of verses; and in churches where a printed service paper is used, it could easily be printed thereon. There is that about antiphonal singing that seems to spur the congregation on to the best efforts possible; no doubt the natural feeling for emulation and competition is partly responsible; but there is in addition the fact that all parts of the congregation have a chance to rest their voices, with the result that when the turn of each section comes round, the allotted verse is attacked with freshness and enthusiasm. Be that as it may, the fact remains that where antiphonal singing has been tried, all are warmly in favour of it, and as a means of spurring on a lukewarm or lethargic congregation, there is no better method."

These are the words of a practical organist and choirmaster; there is nothing in his suggestions that cannot be easily undertaken by any parson and organist who together are not afraid of doing something that has not been done before in their particular church. One of the writers of this present book many years ago found it easy to organize the singing of a London working-class congregation in such a way that some special weekday services and a full Sunday's work (during the absence of the choir on holidays), were sung by the people, the men's and women's voices being used in alternation, and combined in Glorias, doxologies, refrains and final verses of hymns, and so forth. The results included the thrill of which Dr. Thiman speaks ; and nobody seemed to see anything odd in the procedure.

But for congregational singing to become the fine thing it may be, congregational practices are indispensable. Only by such means can the faults that are inevitable in the first singing of an untrained mass be dispelled. Matters of simple discipline are contagious. For example, a congregation without great difficulty may be induced to start a hymn alertly and unanimously by a few minutes of practice and persuasive exhortation devoted to that point. It is not hard to convince them that, so far as aids to preparedness are concerned, they have the same facilities as the choir. Given a familiar tune, hymn-boards, announcements, and playing over of the first line, there is no reason for a single laggard in the nave. Nor have congregations any more excuse than the choir for dragging or being at sixes and sevens; for shouting a verse that clearly ought to be sung quietly ; or for failing to rise to a fervent climax. They have ears and eyes, and the suggestions and stimulations of the organ accompaniment are for them no less than for the choir. Such elementary shortcomings can be cured easily where there is the spirit, and a monthly congregational practice ; hardly otherwise.

The regular practice is necessary, too, when new tunes are to be introduced. Nothing is more likely to prejudice a congregation against a new tune than to introduce it without preparation, especially if it supersedes one that is popular. And it is the finer tunes that are apt to suffer most in this way, because the very qualities that make them fine are apt to be missed at a first hearing, especially when there is in the air a more or less conscious feeling of opposition. Besides, a congregation (especially one that is insistent on its "right" to sing) ought to be no more expected or allowed to "pick up" its new tunes during a service than a choir its anthems. Both choir and congregation need to be reminded that their privileges and rights carry with them obligations and duties ; and the monthly practice for the people ought to be as regular an institution as the weekly practice for the choir.

As to the "when" and "how" of congregational practices : in most churches the half-hour before Evensong will usually be the best time. There may be some distraction due to the arrival of those who are either late for the practice or early for the service ; but the attendance will usually be good because few people object to coming a little earlier for a specific purpose, but many dislike remaining after the service.

For the "how" we must summarise methods that we have personally found successful. The best teaching medium is the conductor's voice, so the first desideratum in the conductor is a voice which he is neither afraid nor unable to raise (more or less pleasantly) in song as well as in speech. Playing over on the organ is far less effective : the use of the instrument is best reserved for a verse when the tune has been pretty well grasped. The position of the conductor depends on the size and acoustics of the building. In a small "dead" church the chancel step is a good place : if there is much echo a short distance down the nave will probably be found better. A roving method is often good, but the conductor who adopts it must beware of speaking with his back to most of the congregation. The less formal and schoolmasterish or ecclesiastical his method, the better. The qualities needed are those with which a good choral society trainer keeps his class alert and interested. Hymn tunes will form the staple of most practices, especially in the early stages ; later may come responses, chanting (but only when at least a portion of the people are provided with psalters, and then always antiphonally in some convenient way) and the congregational parts of the service—the Creed and Gloria to Merbecke or plainsong, etc. Hymns to which descants are sung should be tried, in order that the people may learn to hold to their part ; otherwise some will try to sing the descant, while others will merely listen, some with pleasure, others with annoyance. A few words on any point of historical or musical interest will generally be appreciated.

It is a good plan to begin the practice with a fairly familiar hymn that is to be sung in the ensuing service ; it gives the proceedings a heartening start, and is sound, both educationally and psychologically, proceeding as it does from the known to the unknown, and it induces the right "can do" feeling. A congregation of good average intelligence and musical ability, and supplied at least in part with music editions of the hymn-book, can soon read a new tune after hearing it sung or played once. If the conditions are less favourable, a line at a time is a good method. Words and music alike are more thoroughly taught, and the singers kept on the alert, by some such plan as this (with a four-lined hymn):

> First line of verse 1
> First line of verse 2
> Second line of verse 2
> First two lines of verse 3
> Third line of verse 1
> Fourth line of verse 2
> The whole of verse 4

This may appear to be fussy, but it works, because it spreads the study beyond the first verse; the repetition of the musical phrase to a fresh verbal phrase is good memory-training; and, above all, it keeps the interest alive. Many tunes contain repetitions—*e.g.* line 3 is often a repetition of line 1; in many Welsh eight-lined tunes only four lines have to be learned, the form being: *a.b.a.b.c.d.a.b.*; and the tune to which "Ye watchers and ye holy ones" is sung is an astonishing example of economy, consisting only of two eight-note phrases and one four-note phrase, used at different pitches: *A.A.b.b.C.C.b.b.b.b.* (eight-note phrases represented by capitals). Congregations are always interested in such curiosities of construction, and learn the better for their interest, because the memory is consciously used. The singer who realizes that when he has learned the first line he has also learned the third does something more than make a short cut : he has taken in one of the simplest principles of form—the balancing and answering of phrases.

As we have already said, the congregational chanting of the psalms and canticles presents less difficulty than might be expected, given the assistance of people's copies of psalters. On this point, it is interesting to note that one of the best pleas for congregational chanting occurs in a recently issued symposium, "Manual of Church Praise according to the Use of the Church of Scotland," in a chapter entitled "The Psalter in Worship," by Geo. T. Wright. Mr. Wright admits that prose chanting is not yet popular in Scotland, and probably never will be : the metrical version dies hard. But he argues persuasively on behalf of prose chanting, discussing the use of both plainsong and Anglican chants. And he ends his chapter thus :

> "When the Psalms sing themselves in our minds, however much we loved them before, we shall assuredly love them better still. It is in order to make this possible for all our people that we think ministers and organists and all on whom lies the ordering of the praise of our Scottish Church should seriously consider whether, despite the difficulties attendant upon such a new departure, it were not well that in our Public Worship we should give our people opportunity of chanting the Psalms."

What is thus held to be possible in the Church of Scotland ought to be far from difficult in the Church of England, with its long tradition of prose chanting.

The book just mentioned contains also a capital chapter by Mr. Herbert Wiseman, on congregational practices, wherein methods are discussed at greater length than is possible here. Mr. Wiseman shows that the possibilities of congregational training are far greater than is generally realized. We are interested to note that his experience in Scotland corresponds with that of English conductors of such practices. He rightly emphasizes the advantage of the conductor's voice in "patterning," as against organ, which should be used sparingly ; like ourselves, he has been struck by the impressive effect of *good* soft singing by a congregation (*i.e.*, singing with intensity and the realization of the words and without dragging). People are so often counselled to "sing out." The corresponding command (as already suggested) is needed : "sing in." It can hardly be obtained without practice ; and Mr. Wiseman finds that Scottish congregations, like English, are willing and eager to learn, and of far higher musical intelligence than clergy and organists are apt to realize.

It may reasonably be pointed out that, as organists and choirmasters are notoriously underpaid, the congregational practice adds an additional burden. But it is on all sides an admitted labour of love ; and the time occupied is very short—half an hour monthly (actually less, for the organist would be on the spot ready for Evensong at least ten minutes before the hour) ; and the mutual advantages are not inconsiderable. To many congregations their organist is little more than a name and a music-maker behind a curtain; it is good for both to co-operate in this direct way from time to time. The congregation are led to take an interest in the church's music, with good results on the artistic side, and often on the material as well (the ability shown in a well-conducted congregational practice has been known to attract pupils); and if the choir be brought into the scheme from time to time the occasions serve as wholesome reminders of the duties and obligations of both parties, and so bring about a realization that all present are members both of a congregation and of a choir.

PART III

THE MUSIC: ITS CHOICE AND RENDERING

"I DESIRED oftentimes to witten what was our Lord's meaning. And fifteen year after, and more, I was answered in gostly understanding, seyand thus : woldst thou witten thy Lord's meaning in this thing ? Wete it wele : Love was his meaning. Who shewid it thee ? Love. What shewid he thee ? Love. Wherefore shewid it he ? For Love. Hold thee therein, and thou shalt witten and knowen more in the same."—JULIAN OF NORWICH.

CHAPTER X

CHANTS AND CHANTING

NO attempt can be made to offer detailed guidance
on chanting in this book, either on Anglican or
Gregorian methods. These are helpfully discussed in accessible books and in the prefaces to the
many excellent psalters lately obtainable. A prominent
leader, and a close student of chanting, has recently
exclaimed : "It is really easy to chant properly with
any psalter !" Others, with equal experience, hold that
chanting is the most difficult of all forms of choral art,
and the furthest from attainment. These two statements
are only apparently contradictory : they merely state a
little wildly how unimportant the choice of a psalter is
compared with the grasp of the principles underlying
its use. The basic rulings behind good chanting of the
psalms—rulings of common sense as well as of fitness
and beauty—are, in reality, those which occupied us in
the earlier chapters (III. and IV.). Here we must be
content with suggesting their effectual application to
the psalms, whatever be the form of chant chosen (*i.e.*
whether Gregorian or Anglican, unison or harmonized).

But, no sooner are the above words on paper than
one over-mastering thought comes to mind ; for
it is as clear as the day that, fundamentally, only one
form of chant can ever naturally fit anything with so
decisive and simple a form of its own as the Book of

Psalms. The twofold or antiphonal nature of psalm verses calls for a two-phrase melodic form, and this is to be found both in the Gregorian tone and the Anglican chant. This bond between them is fortunate and unbreakable. It enables them mutually to support each other, and to correct each other's wanderings. The partisans of either, if they will search diligently enough, will find the form they espouse essentially at one, when at its best, with the form they oppose when also at its best. And if the psalms had filled all peoples and languages with the impulse to melodize, and if every nation had its own *Use*, in its own mother-tongue, it seems certain that nature would have given them all this deep derivative likeness, in whatever ways their own particular translations might have diversified the detail. The twofold form would dominate them all. The fling of the first line and the resounding reply of the second, in verse after verse, psalm after psalm, would duly appear in every language, and make the whole world kinsfolk. And here it may be noted that Gregorian and Anglican, as we know them, are more deeply akin than at first appears. They are, indeed, like father and son. To look at the melodic line of the first Gregorian tone, with its second ending, *e.g.*:

and then at the line of an early single chant assigned to Tallis:

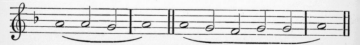

is to see them as parent and child. Or compare Tone VIII., ending I. :

with this more recent Anglican chant :

or Tone V., ending I. :

with this contemporary Anglican example :

It is clear that melodic sophistications, on the one hand, and harmonic, on the other, tend not only to divide them from each other but to make them both less and less amenable to their common purpose.

A second constant and most natural characteristic in the form of the psalms, reflected in both musical uses, must here be noted. In the two-phrase form of verse (or ought we strictly to say in the two-versed stanza ?) the second or fulfilling phrase naturally inclines to be more ample and generally longer than the first. This gives the poems abounding vitality, and it gives the chant the very same quality. For example, in the first verse of the Venite :

"O come, let us sing unto the Lord :
Let us heartily rejoice in the strength of our salvation,"

where "singing" gives place to "hearty rejoicing" and "Lord" grows into "the strength of our salvation," is to be seen the identical creative impulse at work that musically gave the Gregorian tones their expansive endings, and that compelled a four-note phrase to receive a six-note reply in the now stereotyped ten-note single Anglican chant.

Had the Anglican chant remained a unisonal melody, framed at all points to suit the genius of our language and the temper of the people, how much easier it would have been to adapt it—in inflection, pace, volume, disposition—to the spirit and to the ever-varying needs and flexibilities of the psalms themselves ! But, as in plainsong itself, the healthy desire to amplify and beautify the musical utterance brought melodic enrichment with its advantages and dangers, so, from early days, it brought harmonic enrichment to the Anglican chant, with corresponding advantages and dangers. For it brought the need for harmonic design, however slender ; and this, in its turn, induced a new beauty and, with it, a new danger. For, just as only very restrained melodic elaboration is fitted for unskilled worshippers in the case of plainsong, so only very restrained harmonization is suitable in the case of the Anglican chant. And even two such simple harmonic transactions as a half-close at the fourth chord and a full-close at the tenth may induce an unwanted, and even unintended, tinge of *metrical* design. This seems the chief danger-point. And, by something very like bad luck, two good things seem to have combined unhappily to cause English chanting to fall badly before this particular

danger. One of these was the good, working discovery
worshippers made that any simply recurrent metrical
scheme helped their mass-singing to become unanimous.
The other was the creation and popularity of the
metrical paraphrase of the psalms, which tended to make
a correspondingly metrical musical form a thing particularly desired. As time went on, the set single-chant
grew into a double-chant, and became stereotyped as a
species of short-metre hymn-tune. It can at once be
seen that the tendency to harden the chant into a short-
metre tune very soon hinders the true release of the
psalm it is intended to serve, and releases instead a
musical enthusiasm to adorn this set harmonic and
quasi-metrical framework with florid melodic bends and
graces, and so move further and further away from
the sterner mould :

As soon, however, as we revert to this simple basic
form, we find it serves its original purpose aptly, bringing to the psalm an added and wholly unobtrusive
beauty, so long as it is never lazily or inadvertently allowed to degenerate into a set and stony metrical con-
cept. It is precisely this easy-going fall from grace that
has wrought havoc with Anglican chanting, and against
which a great number of church musicians are fighting.

Two main ideas—both in our judgment the result of superficial thinking about unhappy experiences—are in the field against reform ; and they have to be conquered. The first holds that unanimous congregational chanting is impossible without agreed metrical design, not to say a musical metre of agreed rigidity. This has proved itself untrue, for the very good reason that natural accents of fervent utterance always will mean more to an inspired crowd than a metronome ever could mean, and when hearty enough such natural accents will teach them unanimity. The second idea is that singing in harmony is impossible without adding metrical design —that harmony, in fact, is inseparable from ideas of metre and accent. Here, again, the truth (proved in practice over and over again) is otherwise. Chanting in chords can be as beautifully and serviceably flexible as chanting in unison, though it is admittedly less easy.

The accretions of falsehoods round grains of truth are as astonishing as the growth of pearls of great price round a bit of grit in an oyster. But such are nature's ways. Underlying both fallacies are two grains of extractable and admirable truth :

(1) Reliable preconceived metre *does* help congregations to sing together, and always will, provided they can make it their own natural metre.
(2) The ten-note chant *does* need two preconceived points of repose and rallying, and the closes or half-closes this involves (at notes four and ten) resemble metre.

Continuing our analysis of the true and practical nature of the ten-note chant, it is tempting to dogmatize here, and suggest that the moment any metre or quasi-metre offered to a congregation becomes *their metre*, it becomes naturally the much greater and more inspiring thing we call *rhythm*. We must here try to distinguish as exactly as possible between metre and rhythm if we are together to strike the healthy trail for true chanting.

A metrical phrase and a rhythmic phrase are both alike freely chosen groups of notes standing in freely chosen relation with each other. But a metrical phrase is made of an *agreed* number of notes in an agreed relation, while a rhythmic phrase throws notes into a *willed* number and relation. Readers may easily test this fundamental distinction for themselves by listening to the ticking of a clock and quietly singing to themselves these three fragments successively to the uniform tick :

II

The ticking clock is not music, but the three phrases
are. If they are not your choice, but come at you from
without (from some Hymnal Committee who decided
what was good for you!), the clock and its babyish
tunes remain in essence merely metrical, in duple, or
triple or quadruple measures. *The moment you make any
one of these your choice it becomes rhythmical*; and you
will soon find yourself varying the size and volume of
the mechanical tick-note at pleasure. The metre remains intact and helpful as the trellis-work upon which
your rambler roses grow to the advantage of all be-
holders. But no free-born melodists—and the mass
of men are free-born melodists whose education has
been neglected—could leave the above naked and
pre-agreed metre purely metronomic! Metre would
quickly transmute itself to rhythm such as:

Metrical crotchets are like the squares of a chess-board.
Rhythmic crotchets are like nothing mechanical. They
are more like the various men we place on those uniform squares in the course of the freewill game of
melody. There is an immense amount of metrical playing and singing in the world—in brass bands it is most
noticeable: there is too little rhythmic reality. And if
you habitually play or sing thousands of metrical
phrases without transmuting them into your own
rhythms, you will become a metronomical musician.
This is to say, you will be able to chant with the

reliability of the goose-step. But the rhythm of true chanting is another matter altogether. Of all rhythms it is poles asunder from the rhythm of the militarist, which can be a mere metre fatal to the life-rhythm of the individual man.

We may perhaps agree that however much or little prearranged metre is to be allowed in our chanting, it must in all cases fulfil the following three general conditions :

(*a*) It must be such as leaves the congregation free utterance for every speech-rhythm throughout the longest and shortest verses.

(*b*) It must contain just so much agreed accent (or metre) as will draw all voices together at every close and half-close, and give unity to the psalm.

(*c*) It must fulfil the conditions of (*a*) without sacrificing those of (*b*) and *vice versa*.

The major partner in all chanting is the psalm itself. But the musical phrase, junior partner though it may be, exists always to enhance the words. Effectual union is maintained in action chiefly by accentuations which are identical, but also by lengths, and by the suffusion of the willed vocal inflections which constitute the chants themselves, and especially the willed choral cadence of every single verse.

We have distinguished between mere metre and natural rhythm. It is even more necessary to have clear conceptions of the distinction between uniformity and unanimity. Metre that rests on agreed accentuation can secure complete uniformity and some unanimity—

sometimes at a price. But only when *agreed* accentuation becomes *agreeable* to every need of every verse can it rise to rhythm, *i.e.* willed accentuation. This brings complete unanimity with some uniformity. It seems very desirable to make clear to all concerned that, even in Anglican chanting, alert unanimity can be attained with a minimum grain of metrical uniformity. Indeed, it is not too much to say that if it exceeds this minimum of metrical uniformity it soon makes true rhythm and true unanimity impossible in any psalm. Who has not heard the unintelligent, unintelligible, disgraceful hustling of all the words of the so-called recitation into a receptacle-note, made as nearly as possible of a supposititious stock-size semibreve, followed by a senseless elongation or contraction of remaining syllables, small or great, into stock-size minims? There is, perhaps, only one verse in the whole of the psalms which the metrical chant, so disastrously stereotyped, happens to fit for one moment perfectly:

($\downarrow$=112)

Praise him sun and moon: Praise him all ye stars and light.

What of all the other verses? The tyrannous metrical stereotype must go. Congregations, no less than choirs, must be urged to give thought to the whole subject. There is need for a conscious, corporate, complete *disownment* of this degenerate use and conception of the Anglican chant as a mere short-metre tune, tyrannizing over the psalm it sets out to serve. The whole church should put its mind to the question, which is not a purely musical one. And when the present shortcoming has been realized, musicians must plead also for the recognition and restoration of the true uses of the Anglican chant as a fit melody of working flexibility created expressly to give musical wings to the utterance of the psalms in vernacular worship, built therefore to the design of the psalms themselves, like them in two-phrase verses, with a fixed or anchor-accent on the final note of each phrase (*i.e.* on the fourth and tenth notes of the chant).

One word here, in passing, as to the heavy barring of chants still customary. Why should it not be dropped ? It has lately proved itself wholly needless in practice, an encumbrance to the eye of the reader, inducing either hesitation, lumpiness, or a mechanical way of singing. What would a reader of Gray's Elegy say to an edition with every line as heavily barred as our Anglican chant ?

 The | curfew | tolls the | knell of | parting | day.

Put it in front of fifty children and tell them to read it ! The bar-lines of the chant are surely worse than super-fluous. They induce the very defect we most need to avoid. If marks be needed, the horizontal slurs (in common musical use to indicate phrasing) are better than all the bars and double bars :

The fourth and last notes are thus shown as mental anchors, unvarying points of repose and of natural accentuation, coinciding with the final accent of each line of the psalm-verse itself. This fact should give the needed control and the safe flexibility to every phrase in every case. Where this is habitually done, the results are often thrillingly new and varied without ever seeming to get in the least "out of the true." And it is natural this should be so. For, when once the thought of the accent-anchorages becomes a safe habit in the minds of all, the ever-varying speech-rhythms inherent in every verse create ever-varying and equally musical rhythms without confusion.

Let congregations as well as choirs but once catch clear sight of the fundamental difference between the singing of a hymn (or metrical psalm as in Scotland) and the chanting of a psalm, and the battle may be half won. This can be vividly seen if the first verse of Psalm cxxiv. be examined in its two forms. On the musical side there is no more glorious tune than the "Old 124th," and it happens that its first line makes an admirable single chant :

To the metrical paraphrase this metrical hymn-tune is the fitting help-meet. And when once an agreed melody has proved acceptable to the singer, every attendant created thing—words and notes, high and low, strong and weak—and every creative impulse of poet, musician or singer must yield to *it*. Into its mould all utterance is to be poured, and gathered into an inspiring momentous whole :

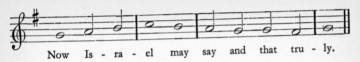

Now Is - ra - el may say and that tru - ly.

This wonder has its own glorious character. It is irresistible. It is a wholly different transaction, as different from true chanting as the final tune of Beethoven's Choral Symphony is from the free recitative that precedes it, or as a military march is from the right hand part of a Chopinesque reverie. How, then, should we *chant* the original words to this very good, ready-made single chant? Here are the words:

"If the Lord Himself had not been on our side, now may Israel say:

"If the Lord himself had not been on our side, when men rose up against us."

and here is the excellent chant:

The following is the clearest picture we can offer of the way *not* to do it:

If the Lord himself had not been on our side   NOW MAY IS-RÁEL SÁY:

If the Lord himself had } SIDE WHEN MÉN ROSE ÚP Á-GAÍNST US.
not been on our }

with a sudden change from unseemly gabble to metrical deliberateness, indicated by the change from small to big type above.

On the other hand, the way in which it will chant itself, if the exultant words are allowed to prevail, might be depicted in approximate notation thus :

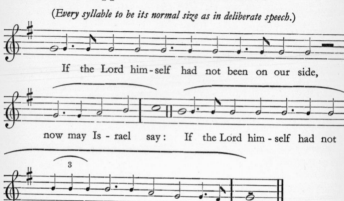

(Every syllable to be its normal size as in deliberate speech.)

If the Lord him-self had not been on our side,

now may Is - rael say : If the Lord him - self had not

been on our side, when men rose up a - gainst us.

To offer all these notes to the singers in every verse is not practical. Nor, happily, is it a necessity. All that is urgently needed is a few pictures in notation of the ever recurring speech-rhythms to put into the mind of the choir concerned a notational approximation to the rhythm which most naturally will emerge as they sing most naturally. This, for example, is a very frequent pattern :

We purposely use the annoyingly vague expression : "Let it 'sing itself.'" For, strange as it may seem, this is what happens with every keen choir, and ultimately (we believe) with the simplest congregational group, *provided* they are keen to try to do it together as perfectly as it can be done ; and we have never once found this keenness fail to respond duly to faithful importunity. All that the singer really needs is a thorough off-by-heart grip of the two phrases :

and then a minimum of marks in the text, *e.g.* thus :

If th. Lord himself had not been on oúr síde, nów may ¹ Israel say :

If the Lord himself had nót béen on our síde, when | men rose ¹ up a- | gainst us.

There are many methods of marking. The above is but one of them. The reader may devise improved markings for his choir. The accents on certain syllables are marks of natural rallying points, to be put in here and there if needed.* The dots beneath a syllable are most useful for indicating natural shortness. Then the vertical ticks or "bars" are an absolute need in all verses at points where the inflective melody begins to move to its final note.

All unnatural hustling of noble words or elongation of unimportant ones is fatal to sense and to reverence. Sensitive metre is a friend, but senseless metre can kill sensitive rhythm. No such crime is for

* Bridges thought it wise and helpful to choirs to mark what he called colliding accents, as at the words "not been" above.

a moment to be tolerated, still less deemed an Anglican necessity. It is a mere lazy, metrical makeshift for the rhythmic reality. Any village choir, in earnest to express the beauty and meaning of the psalm, is demonstrably able to unify utterance on the living rhythms of the psalms. They have but to think of the chant as the free melody it is, consisting of two short phrases, safely anchored to their final notes :

and flexibility will result. In all cases, however, they must agree on signs which all can recognize where the changes of note occur ; and in all cases their fourth and tenth notes must coincide with the final verbal accent of the verse and half verse. For the rest they will find by study together that the speech-rhythms which are most natural to them will fashion for them an infinitely varied series of natural music-rhythms *that need never hurt the melody they are using*, all lying within the two-phrase chant. It is, by the way, ever to be remembered that the converse is not true, and that a badly chosen chant *may* hurt an all-important verse of a psalm, while suiting other verses. For this reason no chant should be chosen for any psalm that does not fit and give due life to its every verse.

In connection with the necessity noted in the last sentence, we must now try, before turning to the question of Gregorian chanting, to offer a little homely advice as to the problems of choice and practice of harmonized Anglican chants. To deal with the latter

point first, we strongly recommend all choirs and singing congregations to conceive chanting as harmonious
and inflected reading rather than singing; and, with this
always at the back of the mind, to adopt the following
method of practice in the early stages (and long after !):

    (i) Read the first verse together ; then
  (ii) Monotone it together exactly as read.
 (iii) Sing it together on a single chord (the final
          chord of the chant chosen).
 (iv) Sing it inflected to the full chant, making the
          paces and the rhythms approximate in all
          four processes.

The reading (i) and the singing needs (iv) have to be
reconciled. This will cause the reading to become deliberate, and the singing will seem to become swift by
comparison. Both will gain greatly in clearness and
intensity. Read singingly. Sing readingly. As practice
proceeds, it will not be necessary for the team to do
more than

    (i) Recite on the key-chord alone ;
  (ii) Sing readingly to the whole chant.

As to choice of chants for each psalm, this rests with
leaders, yet a good deal of genial committee work will
be found possible and useful. Our stress laid upon
Tallis in this chapter may be in danger of suggesting
that "back to the old" is our advocacy. By no means.
We would rather say "on to the new," such, *e.g.*, as this :

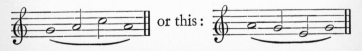

It is indeed astonishing that such exquisitely beautiful phrases of primal simplicity should still be awaiting discovery and use for English chanting! The possible permutations of a ten-note melody run into millions. Of these, probably thousands are beautiful. We venture in truth neither to advocate new or old. Is the following new or old?

We have not a notion of its origin. It is beautiful. Its gentleness of inflection reminds one of the verses:

> "Lord, thou art become gracious unto thy land :
>   thou hast turned the captivity of Jacob.
> Thou hast forgiven the offence of thy people :
>   and covered all their sin."

It, and hundreds like it (that a very child might discover), go well to such a psalm ; and the more simply they are matched with harmony the better. Would that we could all think and use the inspired melodies of old (as already suggested) as though the ink were not dry upon the first copy made of them! Would that we could all equally think of and use inspired chant melodies of yesterday and today as though they had merely waited discovery since before the world began! When we can do this, controversy on such matters will be duly ashamed of itself. Inspired melody is obviously never a thing of the past. It must be the discovery of a million todays, whether composed a century or a single minute ago ; each generation must newly discover the

old chant for its newness and venerate the brand new
for its potential antiquity. We counsel our readers to
view this vital matter clearly. The grace of line in a
good chant, new or old, reminds us of the finer lines
of a beautiful countenance. "How like those that have
gone!" we exclaim; and they are sometimes hardly
distinguishable; yet each has its own character written
clear in the salient lines; delightful to contemplate;
variable though constant. If a good chant be thought
of in this way, good choice fitted to the character of
each psalm will be more ensured.

Let us, in conclusion of this section, admit that
musicians with more zeal for the music than for the
words are apt to put musical interests first, and then
chants are apt to grow wild. Some grow as amazing
as they are inept, developing into reminders of what
used to be called "pretty little tunes for pretty little
players," or into perverse musical exercises such as
the conceits called *recte et retro*—chants, that is, that go
first forward, then in the second half backward, chord
by chord. A playful chant used in the boyhood of the
present writer at St. George's, Windsor, runs as follows :

It was sung under Elvey to "When Israel came out
of Egypt," and well to "The mountains skipped like

rams," but became inadequate at "Tremble, thou earth."
Here, again, is a complacent sort of chant:

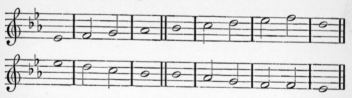

Is there any psalm that could bear such a trite companion? These are only named here as chants that
may defeat their use as *means* by thinking of themselves as *ends*, however ingenious or amiable they
may be, or congenial to this or that mind, *qua* musical
affairs.

The psalms offer infinite melodic scope. If exuberant
verses claim exuberant melodies to match, it is imperative that all solemn or quiet verses that may occur
in the course of an exuberant psalm should be given a
solemn or sedate melody. If a psalm has many moods
and but one chant is desirable, it must be a strain so
plain, so reticent in itself, that no mood can be belied
by it, yet all held in unity by it, the singers reflecting the
varying moods, as is ever right, by fit choice and varia-
tion of speed, spacing, light and shade.

Plainsong chanting has difficulties of its own, but
there is, we think, a tendency to exaggerate them. The
fact (we believe it to be a fact) that England is the only
country where plainsong is used with the vernacular
seems to have led some writers to over-estimate the
difficulty of applying to English a series of inflections
devised for Latin. But the thing can be done, and with

CHANTS AND CHANTING 175

beautiful effect. The subject, however, needs special study, and cannot be dealt with in a page or two of a work on church music in general. The bibliography names some authoritative treatises, and the study of one or more of these should be supplemented by instruction from an organist whose choir shows his practical grasp of the subject. There are few large centres without at least one church where plainsong is understood; and opportunities of instruction occur in plenty at Summer Schools and in connection with the School of English Church Music. It is unfortunate that the experts differ on some points. A safe guide is "The Elements of Plainsong": it presents the purist's view, but without narrowness, though not always without preciosity. We refer the reader to such textbooks, and restrict ourselves here to a few observations, some of a warning nature, on points concerning the use of plainsong in parish churches.

First, as to the bogey of "correctness": we venture to say that the cause of plainsong in the country has suffered from a failure to realize that what is suitable in a monastery is not always—or indeed often—suitable in a parish church. The refinements of monastic singing are the result of years of study and daily singing of nothing else but plainsong; the consistent use of the half-voice, varied only by the pianissimo endings, and the modal harmonies played mostly on manuals only, with a light stop or two, though suitable and beautiful in a community chapel, would be exotic, even if attainable, in an average parish church. And here let us declare ourselves to be heretics concerning some of the notions of the purists as to performance. In doing so we feel we are expressing the views of many musicians who, like ourselves, concede all that is claimed for plainsong as a distinct form of musical art, and one of great beauty. But there is an aspect of the question that is apparently too little considered by those who are plainsong experts rather than practical musicians, and it is in this respect that organists who are musicians and not plainsong specialists need a few words of counsel.*

Although plainsong is a type of music independent of the measured type from which modern music has developed, it is still music, and, as such, its performance is not exempt from fundamental principles that (being based on common-sense) apply to all music alike. When, therefore, the purist says that the final words of every verse of a psalm must be "properly sustained and sung pianissimo," in order to produce "the right effect of restfulness,"† his dictum must be challenged. Among the worst faults of interpretation are monotony and conventionality; to apply so pronounced a musical effect as a pianissimo to every verse-end in a long psalm, regardless of the general character of the psalm, the particular character of its verses, and the relative importance of the final accented word, seems to us both conventional and monotonous, and an unspiritual use of music. Moreover, whatever arguments may be

* *Mutatis mutandis*, what follows applies to the performance of plainsong in general, although we have in view especially that fitted for congregational use.

† "Elements of Plainsong."

brought forward on behalf of an impersonal use of the psalter, the fact remains that the psalms are amongst the most personal poems in existence. The last thing to be desired is a descriptive method of singing and accompaniment; but the vivid contrasts (often in the course of a few verses), and the blend of drama, emotion, and reflection, that make the psalter one of the most diversified of books can never be disregarded with impunity. In our view there is no justification for ignoring the natural differences of pace and power called for by strongly contrasted psalms. Can it be devotionally or musically right to sing (say) the *Jubilate Deo* and the *Miserere mei* at exactly the same pace, with the half-voice, and ending every verse pianissimo? Both instinct and devotion, alike religious and musical, would demand quite other treatment of such refrains as "Set up Thyself, O God," "For his mercy endureth for ever," "O that men would therefore praise the Lord," "O put thy trust in God," and so forth. The "effect of restfulness" fitting in a monastic house may, on being transplanted to a parish church, become mere drowsiness.

A feature on which the purist lays great stress is the pause at the colon: an old rule, we are told, was that "it should be long enough to say 'Ave Maria.'"* We have heard zealots for the pause demand even a three-fold repetition of Ave Maria; and certainly the break is often long enough to interpolate so much, provided the invocation be smartly uttered—a fact which shows that the employment of words as a time-measure may

* "Elements of Plainsong."

be risky. "A good pause at the colon gives dignity to the chanting."* We have yet to be convinced that anything more than the customary full breath is necessary; and there is nothing dignified in a systematically pronounced silent pause *per se*. Used sparingly, with firsthand purpose, silence can be more eloquent and more devout than speech or song. Moreover, the silent pause is one of the most arresting of musical effects; but its occurrence in every verse becomes both monotonous and affected—even when it is entirely unanimous, which is by no means always the case. We have sometimes asked for a solid practical argument on behalf of this feature, and the only answer that went beyond a mere statement that "they do it at Solesmes" claimed that it brought out the parallelism of the verses. But the parallelism is already defined by the use of the colon as a full breath-mark. Moreover, although the parallelism is the main constructional feature of the psalms, it is far from being constant. In many isolated but important instances where there is no parallelism, the effect of the colon is to break the sense—especially in short verses that can be sung easily in one breath. We see neither dignity nor common-sense in accentuating the break in such verses as "Lord, lift Thou up : the light of Thy countenance upon us"; "Whoso doeth these things : shall never fail"; "Let the words of my mouth and the meditation of my heart : be alway acceptable in Thy sight"; "O Lord : my strength and my redeemer"; and in many others that readily come to mind. Indeed, the colon is so often a badly placed disruptive feature that

* "Elements of Plainsong."

there is much to be said for a method of pointing that
shifts or ignores it, as the "English Psalter" does with
good effect. The "good pause at the colon" needs
far better justification than has so far been brought
forward.

As to accompaniment: this should undoubtedly be
modal, or at least diatonic, which is not necessarily the
same thing. Perhaps this distinction may usefully be
made clear by a single and simple example: It is easy
to harmonize the plainsong tune "Pange Lingua"
("E. H.," No. 326) in the key of C throughout, save
for the concluding chord, which would be the "final"
of the mode—a chord of E minor (or major). The difference between this diatonic method and the right
modal way may be most easily shown by these two
harmonizations:

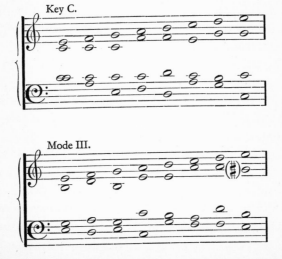

Plainsong accompaniment should generally consist of simple progressions—common chords and first inversions. But there are occasions when this simple basis may be fittingly elaborated by the use of passing notes and diatonic dissonances—the dominant seventh, however, being rarely, if ever, touched. Chords may be changed during the recitation, such changes taking place on an accented syllable ; and much may be done by contrasting a gently moving organ part with the vocal monotone of the recitation ; and, on the other hand, during the mediation and ending, by a sustained organ part against which the vocal inflection moves as passing notes. The vocal part should not, as a rule, be duplicated in the top line of the accompaniment. The whole of the organ part may effectively be placed above the voices, quiet stops only being used. The plainsong may be used as a bass of the accompaniment. The texture of the organ part may vary from two-part harmony (or even a single line of counter-melody) to widespread full chords (not necessarily loud). The possibilities are almost infinite. There is, in fact, a world of beauty in this by-path of music that is rarely explored, mainly because textbooks inevitably do little more than exemplify the bases. The best accompaniment is a matter of improvisation, not of the printed page, and proficiency calls for long study and experience. It will then be seen that the simplest type need not be dull, nor its development distracting. As to power : the antiphony of cantors and full, or boys and men, will permit—even demand—ample contrast which need, however, be neither violent nor restless in effect.

Unaccompanied plainsong in a resonant building is satisfyingly beautiful, and it should therefore be so sung on occasion, and for that reason, *not* (as the purist maintains) merely because it was unaccompanied in the early days of the church. The reason for unaccompanied singing in the primitive church was the prosaic one that organs were few and far between, and on the few that existed the player (or literally the thumper—*pulsator organorum*) could do little more than deliver the notes of the chant. As soon as organs became frequent and more tractable, accompaniment became general. At the beginning of the plainsong revival in England, it became chromatic too, the result being a dreadful hybrid that is not yet quite extinct. We have no quarrel with the Solesmes enthusiasts so far as harmonic simplicity is concerned ; but we see no point in an accompaniment that must be "small in volume," "reduced to a minimum," "unobtrusive," or used merely as "a support to the voice."* To take the last point first, choirs unable to sing unsupported should leave plainsong alone, seeing that, according to Solesmes, it must be sung throughout with half-voice and with an ever-recurring pianissimo—both effects demanding either skilled singers or a prohibitive amount of practice. As to "unobtrusiveness," plainsong accompaniment, like any other kind, should surely justify itself as a thing of rare beauty, "to the good" in worship, adorning the plainsong without drowning it or interfering with the flow of the chanting. In short, if the psalms are to be sung, whether to plainsong or to

* "Elements of Plainsong."

modern chants, we fail to see why both voices and organ are to be reduced to a perpetual mezzo-piano, regardless of the character of the text.*

Another point on which the parish church organist should not allow himself to be over-Solesmesed, so to speak, is in the treatment of the Gloria Patri. The "correct" use is to regard it merely as a couple of verses of the psalm, to be sung antiphonally. But in effect this often leads to an anti-climax. For example, when the antiphony is between cantor and choir, the second half of the Gloria may fall to a single voice. The effect is never good; we have known instances where, the cantor being feeble, the ending to a jubilant psalm has been almost ludicrous. Even when the psalms are sung by boys and men in alternation, there is something inconclusive about an ending by boys alone. We have never heard an argument in favour of this method, which overlooks the obvious fact that the Gloria Patri is not a part of the psalm but a Christianizing appendix; and as a doxology it clearly ought to be treated as a chorus, and with a due degree of power.

The plainsong methods we have questioned—the monotonous use of the half-voice, the unduly long break at the colon, the characterless accompaniment, the frequent anticlimax due to the antiphonal treatment of the Gloria Patri, and, above all, the infliction of monotonous uniformities—are all opposed to the

* A consistently quiet treatment of such choir-music as the Introit (among which are some of the loveliest examples of pure melody in existence) is, however, called for by the character of the music, which often suggests a solo voice or semichorus.

primary laws of musical interpretation, and they are
no more tolerable in plainsong than in any other kind
of music. And at long last, even when due admira-
tion has been given to the Solesmes monks for their
patient and valuable research, the fact remains that
some of their findings are admittedly no more than
conjecture.

If plainsong is to be used by ordinary people, the
accent should be shifted to the second syllable—song.
Song is something to be sung; its performance should
be (1) vitally related to the text with which it is associated, and (2) subject to the inspiring tenets of good
natural singing. Plainsong has its own rhythm, its own
modal system, and no musician with a sense of beauty
will do anything to damage either; but he may well
question its right to any methods of performance
today that are not based on universally accepted and
acceptable principles.

The new and growing use of this ancient and beautiful music, if only it be vital and reasonably fitting, is to
be welcomed as one of the most beneficent influences in
church music today. Its adoption will become more
general with a fuller realization both of its idiomatic
differences from, and its spiritual affinity to, the best
church music of later periods. But we are constrained to warn our fellow-enthusiasts in the cause
of true chanting that few, if any, normal choirs and
congregations will be able to sing plainsong in the
manner of the monks of Solesmes. Even if they
could they wouldn't; for to them plainsong will not
be a subtle and delicate antique, to be sung *sotto voce*

and accompanied on the organ's softest stop (which is surely what is meant by "reducing the accompaniment to a minimum"); it will be just a simple and beautiful kind of church music, to be sung, as we may be sure it was sung centuries ago, with both vitality and variety.

CHAPTER XI

HYMNS AND HYMN SINGING

AS the nature of hymn melodies has already occupied us in considering congregational singing in Chapter IX., we begin our discussions here with a glance at the resources of today, because so great a wealth of material carries with it both problems and responsibilities, besides being bound up with the burning question of choice of tunes, which often means the dropping of old friends in favour of possible new ones.

It is a truism that modern hymnals are too large, yet there is ample justification for bulk. John Wesley's ideal book, described in his "Preface to a Collection of Hymns for use of the People called Methodists" (1779), is now impossible : "What we want is, a Collection not too large, that it may be cheap and portable ; nor too small, that it may contain a sufficient variety for all occasions." What would he have said to the 1933 successor of his Collection ? It contains nine hundred and eighty-four hymns, and well over a thousand tunes, besides chants, etc., the whole filling a thousand and forty-two pages. Somebody has said that the perfect hymnal, when it comes, will contain no more than about a couple of hundred hymns ; and no doubt that number represents approximately the total of hymns and tunes that have won universal acceptance. But it is also true that the hymns—and even more emphatically the tunes

—concerning which people feel most strongly are the many hundreds that the perfect hymnal will not include. Nobody grows warm about the standard tunes ; they are, in fact, so taken for granted that the omission of, say, "St. Anne," from a new hymnal would cause surprise rather than indignation. It is otherwise with tunes that may be called favourite rather than classic. "Eventide," "St. Anatolius," "Hollingside," "Melita," "Nicæa," "St. Columba," "Abends," "St. Clement," "Maidstone," "Regent Square," "Golden Sheaves," "St. Gertrude," "Aurelia," and a hundred others of the kind, chiefly by the composers that made "A. & M." an epochal book : to omit these is to raise a storm of protest from all sorts of people. A hymn-book is an anthology, and it must be inclusive rather than exclusive. This being so, it must take into account, not only the contemporary output, but also the revival of old tunes. One of the best features in modern hymnals is the prominence given to eighteenth-century tunes that had almost been forgotten. To the compilers of the original "A. & M." such tunes, no doubt, seemed secular, or savouring of dissent ; today they are widely enjoyed for their melodious and singable character, and (not least) for their Englishness. A few examples come to mind at once—"Richmond," "Mount Ephraim," "University," "Retirement," and many others that were popular in the old "west gallery" days. But the chief reason why compilers of hymnals now cast their nets wide is that they cannot ignore the present move towards improvement in church music. The reformers may sometimes have been tactless and over-zealous, but there can be no denying the steady improvement that has been wrought in church music, and in no department more than in hymnody—the one most difficult to tackle, because of its popularity. Practically every hymn-book produced during the past twenty years has, in a greater or less degree, played its part in the reform movement, and it has usually done so in the only common-sense way, *i.e.* by including good new (or revived old) tunes as alternatives to popular and inferior examples. This has involved a very large increase of material—an increase that may be only temporary. For the supersession of a bad tune by a good one seems to be an affair of three stages : first, the two appear side by side ; next, the inferior tune is relegated to the appendix ; and, finally, it is dropped. Stages one and two are exemplified in the two editions of the "English Hymnal." In the 1933 edition over a hundred tunes have been added, room being made for them by the dropping of duplicates and the placing of about fifty others in the Appendix. As a large proportion of the fifty are from Victorian sources, we may expect to see the next edition dropping them altogether. If the tunes that take their place were obviously superior, nobody would complain of that; but it is difficult to resist an impression that most of the substitutes, though entirely free from sentimentality, are also deficient in appeal and singableness ; and some of them are so markedly in the fashion of today that they will soon be as much out of date as the Victorians whose place they have taken.

In the matter of hymns, hymn-tunes, and hymn-singing, the church musician will do well to remember that the views of the more intelligent type of layman may be considered with profit, on account of the extra-musical considerations involved.

Let us take, for instance, two public utterances that may be held to express the views of a considerable proportion of church folk. The first was an article in a daily paper on "The Choice of Hymns" by a dean who was formerly headmaster of a famous public school—where, no doubt, he had ample opportunity of observing the type of hymn and tune that "goes."

He began by saying what a good many of us have felt for some time past : "It is fashionable today to sneer at 'Hymns Ancient and Modern,' and I should myself prefer the 'English Hymnal' ; but I think the fashionable abuse is largely undeserved."

After discussing the important part played by association (a point too little considered by compilers of hymn-books), he goes on : "I am not a blind admirer of the 'English Hymnal.' I am infuriated on every occasion when they suggest that I should sing the ungrammatical sentence, 'Hail thee, festival day !' ; and there is plenty in it to criticize. But it certainly marks a great advance. Still, I shall always be grateful to 'Hymns Ancient and Modern' for having shown the way, for having introduced me to many good and some beautiful hymns, and for having for the first time done something to show the wealth of singable religious poetry which the nation possesses."

This is in pleasant contrast to the attitude adopted by reformers in a hurry, who are apt to forget the gratitude that is always due to a pioneer. After all, when one book has shown the way, it is not hard for a second one to come along and improve on its predecessor in regard to weaknesses that were due to the taste of the period rather than to the shortcomings of the compilers. Moreover, most of the sweeping opponents of "Ancient and Modern" do not take into account the edition of 1904, which is free from many of the faults of previous editions. In fact, some of its excellences caused its comparative failure : it made too big a break with convention, and (to name one important point) its hymns for mission services do not include one example of the trivial, sentimental type—a detail in which the "English Hymnal" shows surprising weakness.

The other article on the subject was entitled "Hymns: Problems of Verse and Tune," by a well-known novelist. This is what he had to say concerning the latter :

"The tune must always be a terrible problem. I wish I had means of judging how the changes of taste particularly, which the authors of 'Songs of Praise' aimed at inaugurating, are really working out in practice. What they gave us was better than anything we had before, and we cannot be too grateful to them ; but what they gave was still only a contribution and it had conspicuous faults. On the literary side, the search for poetry went too far and wide ; we find congregations invited to sing together words that hardly suggest song at all—even in the less exacting conditions of private life ; while a particular smack of taste, a flavour of sufficiency deriving in part from folk-song worship and in part from a dryish sacerdotalism, tends

to domineer in the music, and is, I think, already
dated."

We think there is much in this : many of the new
tunes that are too obviously influenced by folk-song and
the ecclesiastical modes begin to show signs of wear ;
a decade or so hence they will probably be superseded
either by another and more natural type of new tune, or
(perhaps even more likely) by a reinstatement of the
best of the nineteenth-century tunes they were intended
to displace.

As to the use of folk-tunes for hymn purposes : there
are two main tests—quality, and freedom from too
obviously secular associations. Can it be said that all—
or even the majority—of those pressed into service in
modern hymnals pass both ? High quality may excuse
some hazard in regard to the second test, because the
secular associations are transitory—often, indeed,
merely local. The secular origin of some of the best-
loved of German chorales has long been forgotten ;
and the splendid risk taken when a mediæval love-song
became the Passion chorale and "Innsbruck, I now must
leave thee" was sacredly parodied into "O world, I
now must leave thee," and gave "Innsbruck" to the
Church, has been amply justified. The incorporation
of an unquestionably fine folk-tune into a hymnal is,
then, valuable salvage work. But the glamour of the
"folk" origin of an air ought not to offset characteristics
that, however desirable in an unaccompanied solo song,
may become fatal defects in a hymn-tune. Had some
of the more jingling of the "English Hymnal" folk-
melodies occurred in a set of nursery rhymes by the

Rev. John Bacchus Dykes they would at once have been recognized for what they are—examples of mere complacent tunery, so to speak.

The folk-tune vogue will pass in hymnals, as already it has almost passed in composition; and it is becoming plain that many of the new tunes are less good than they appeared to be, and that certain of the old ones are less bad than we were led to believe. On this point our novelist says:

> I rather resent not being allowed the familiar tune of "Eternal Father, strong to save," with that fierce rush in the bass. Is it so bad? I liked it when I was a boy. I like it now.

He need not be ashamed of his liking for "Melita": plenty of musicians still regard it as a good tune, despite the melodic weakness in the fifth line brought about by the rising semitones. Above all, it has one great merit in a hymn-tune—it really "goes," and congregations of all kinds sing it. The tune that displaces it in "Songs of Praise" is a folk-song with a charm of its own. But, as "strength" is the quality our reformers demand in hymn-tunes, it has to be pointed out that "Lodsworth" is *not* strong. However, its chief weakness is its repetitiveness. This is a good example of the ease with which distinguished musicians may miscalculate in compiling hymn-books. There can be little doubt that, judged purely from the melodic point of view, "Lodsworth" is superior to "Melita." It has a better "line"; and there is a climax. But when we look elsewhere than at its melodic curve, we soon see why it may be an excellent folk-song and a poor hymn-tune. In addition to the monotony brought about by its repetitiveness, there is a kindred defect in its implications of cadences. Folk-songs are independent of harmony: hymn-tunes are not. Even an unaccompanied melody can no longer be judged purely on its merits as a tune in rise and fall: our people to-day are aware of its harmonic implications. So we cannot be deaf to the fact that of the six lines of "Lodsworth," five end on the tonic and one on the supertonic. "Eternal Father" consists of four six-lined verses, so a little arithmetic will show how many times we hear the same chord.

We discuss this tune at some length, because it is only one of a good many instances of folk-song being employed as hymn-tunes without due consideration. No wonder the novelist critic asks if "Melita" is, after all, a bad tune. The answer is that it is not bad, nor is it very good, but that, as a setting for the words, and as material for congregational singing, it beats "Lodsworth" all ends up. Why, then, was it dropped in "Songs of Praise" and relegated to the Appendix in the "English Hymnal"? The answer is easy: It is trebly damned: (1) it was a popular "A. & M." tune; (2) it was Victorian; and (3)—and worst of all—it was by a composer whose name in "reforming" circles has become almost a synonym for meretriciousness.

When all is said (much of it justly) in deploration of Victorian tunes, it is surprising to discover how many are still indispensable. Even the new edition of the "English Hymnal" contains nearly a hundred, for example. Will the 1990 edition contain as many of the

folk-songs and modal tunes of the neo-Georgians?
What is the secret of the success of the best of the old
"Ancient and Modern" tunes? It used to be said that
they owed their popularity to a few luscious chords;
there was a good deal in that, so far as Dykes and
Barnby were concerned, but we doubt if their detractors
have ever taken sufficiently into account their far more
important quality of *singableness*. Some of them may
be poor to play, or even to listen to when sung; but
hymn-tunes are for singing rather than for hearing.
Again, their rhythm was unenterprising, it is true; still,
this defect is one that is more apparent to the listener
than to the singer. But an unenterprising rhythm is
also a rhythm without traps: too many new tunes contain rhythmic and structural schemes that are striking, ingenious, unusual, interesting—but which are pitfalls for
a congregation, except in places where congregational
practices are held, or where there is a strong choir that
really *leads* in hymn singing (not all strong choirs do).

Similarly, archaisms in harmony and melody may give
keen pleasure to musicians; but they mean little or
nothing to the layman, who, indeed, is likely to be put
off by them. And even musicians find that archaisms
don't always wear well, and soon reveal a touch of
preciosity.   *Fastidious refinement, esp. in language*

In thus controverting the controverters of "Hymns
A. & M.," our one desire is to offer such timely
stimulus as we can to the appreciation of that admirably
serviceable work. The Church cannot be too mindful
of its debt. But we yield to none in our gratitude for
the breath of fresh air which the "English Hymnal"

and (at about the same time) the 1904 and 1909 (Historical) editions of "Hymns A. & M.," both brought into the hymn-tune world. We deplore equally what we believe to be the melodic affectations of the new school and the harmonic weaknesses of the old. Excesses mar both, as excess always must mar the music of the Church. The choice of chords for their own sweet sake was bad ; is the choice of melodies on the ground of their "folk" or other origin, rather than of their intrinsic merit or suitability, any better ? Our hope and belief is that a risen taste, in debt to both, will choose and demand the best of both, and future hymnals will consummate their excellences.

*   *   *   *   *

The first impression one gets as a result of much experience in churches of various types, is that the admirable enterprise shown by the compilers of recent hymnals is not imitated by the users. Investigation would probably show that the choice of hymns in a normal parish church is surprisingly limited. There are, for example, many fine things in the "English Hymnal" that we, personally, have never, or very rarely, heard sung, during the thirty years of the book's existence. Now, as popular taste is most directly influenced by the songs and hymns that people sing communally, it is clear that the possibilities for good presented by contemporary hymn-books are not being developed. At present the favourite hymn of the parson, the organist, the choir, or of some influential parishioner, is too prominent in the music lists. Instead, there ought to be a regular system of adding to the repertory ; where congregational practices are held, a new hymn—even two—should be learned on every occasion ; and the hymns so learned should be used fairly frequently during the ensuing month or two, in order that they may become established. The choice of hymns is generally made by the parson *or* the organist : it should be a joint affair, the ecclesiastical and musical sides being alike safeguarded. This co-operation will make it easy to extend the repertory. The organist should always have ready a few fine things of differing types, suitable for various seasons and occasions, and should work them in judiciously. In drawing up the monthly music list for the parish magazine, the people's musical part should be as carefully considered, not only for its fitness, but for its variety and appeal, as the music for the choir. How often is it ?

Note that word "appeal." There are two wrong ways of using such a treasury of new and old as the "English Hymnal." The first is to disregard both new and old, and to stick to the familiar numbers that are in practically every hymnal. The second is to make too little use of the familiar, and to choose largely from the most difficult, antique, and austere examples of which the "English Hymnal" contains perhaps rather too many. This fault is not common, but it exists in varying degrees, and always with unfortunate results. We know at least one church that was emptied in six months by the introduction of the "English Hymnal" and its maladroit use by a parson who held the view that the fitness of a hymn-tune was shown by its differing in as many respects as possible from those that made "Ancient and Modern" the most popular of hymnals. All his choices were no doubt intended to be fitting, but few made any appeal to ordinary folk. And in this connection the chooser of hymns, as of every kind of music for popular use, needs to remind himself constantly that there are many kinds of good music; that in some of them the goodness is discernible only by the trained musician; in others by some sort of specialist; in yet others by the crowd—but only on thorough acquaintance. Finally, and happily, there is the kind of musical goodness that makes instant appeal to the untrained no less than to the trained musician. The music of which this may be said is truly universal; it is enormous in quantity, and it embraces every type, from the symphony to the simple organ voluntary, from the oratorio to the Anglican chant. Popular musical education must begin with such things. Parsons and organists with a taste for medieval melodies, Genevan psalm tunes, and German chorales are apt to forget that their liking for such things is usually the result of long familiarity or of special study. They must not expect their congregations to share their delight at once—if ever.

Although unison singing is desirable in the congregation, it may easily be overdone in the choir. For a choir consists of more or less trained voices of varying compass, and tenors and basses alike are reasonable in objecting to long stretches of singing at a pitch that is too low for the one and too high for the other. Long processional hymns in unison, unless very moderate in compass, are a real infliction on the choir: the alternation of boys' (and women's) voices and men's is an improvement, but the result is apt to be monotonous unless the organist is able to vary the harmonies. The best arrangement in a long procession is a mixture of harmony (unaccompanied, if possible), unison, boys, men, with free accompaniment, and occasional short interludes.

This question of tenor and bass compass has been too little considered in hymn-books that adopt a pitch suitable for the congregation. In the "English Hymnal," for example, the pitch is often so low that the basses are at times working hard with barely audible results, and the tenors are restricted to their least effective register. Let the convenience of the congregation be considered, by all means ; but the choir should not be forgotten, especially as a very slight rearrangement of the parts will often solve the difficulty.

Mention has been made of free organ accompaniment of unison singing. This is far from easy, demanding not only a thorough knowledge of harmony and considerable technical skill, but also some of the ready invention of the improvisor. At its best it is of great effect. Our bibliography contains some works on the subject that will be useful.

Just as the immense resources of modern hymnals are still barely tapped, so the potentialities of hymn-singing are rarely realized to the full ; and probably the facts are not unrelated. A plain service containing no other music than a few fine hymns, heartily sung by all, lacks nothing of dignity or beauty ; and when this hearty congregational hymn-singing occurs in a service at which more elaborate, but not less worthy music is well sung by the choir, both types gain from the contrast. But both must be equally good in their different ways, and no doubt the objections made to choir music are often based on some lack of effectiveness due to the absence of this contrasting of the massed singing with that of a skilled choir. An example of this value—not to say necessity—of contrast is shown in cathedrals, where congregational hymn-singing is now encouraged instead of being frowned on as it seems to have been formerly. The singing of a cathedral choir is never more delightful than when it is thrown into relief by some congregational hymns. *Per contra*, a first-rate choir and a half-silent congregation may produce a chilling effect.

For the rest, there is no better advice than that of John Wesley in his "Directions to Singers." He had choir-singers in mind, but most of his advice applies equally to congregations.

"Sing *All*. . . . Let not a slight degree of weakness or weariness hinder you. If it is a cross to you, take it up, and you will find it a blessing.

"Sing *lustily* and with a good courage.

"Beware of singing as if you are half dead, or half asleep, but lift up your voice with strength. Be no more afraid of your voice now, nor more ashamed of its being heard, than when you sing the songs of *Satan*.

"Sing *modestly* . . . strive to unite your voices together so as to make one clear melodious sound.

"Sing *in time* . . . and take care not to sing too slow. This drawling way naturally steals on all who are lazy ; and it is high time to drive it from among us, and sing all our tunes just as quick as we did at first.

"Above all, sing *spiritually*. Have an eye to God in every word you sing . . . attend strictly to the sense of what you sing, and see that your *heart* is not carried away with the sound, but offered to God continually."

CHAPTER XII

AT THE COMMUNION

PROBABLY at no point is music in so great a danger of hindering the worship which it expressly sets out to help as in the Divine Office—whether the music be that of the most elaborate choral celebration, or of the humblest service of the "Lord's Supper" (as it is often named in the Free Churches), or in the varying orders and grades of services of Holy Communion which lie between those two extremes. It is clear that in so vast a range of possible utterance—from the elaborate choral settings down to the corporately spoken word (which often, by the way, drops to barely more than a confused murmur) —the range of responsible choice and the dangers of possible offence, whether by redundance or short-coming, are equally vast.

There are devout worshippers who find their worship hindered by any elaborate efforts of choir and organ; and there are also musical churchmen sincerely concerned who would desire no music at all in this service. These people deserve mindful regard from their musical servants. No one can justify or uphold the use of music or any other thing that draws the well-disposed worshipper's attention to itself, at this of all services. On the other hand, who would forbid its use, if it enhances and intensifies the innermost end

of the service itself? True we may not unsafely attribute some part of the devout worshippers' shrinking
from music to the *bad* usage of *good* music; though
some must be due also to painstaking usage of intolerably self-important music.

Whatever music is right and fitting for this solemn
service, it must never fail to fulfil three general conditions:

(1) It must be such music as is intelligible to the
congregation present;

(2) It must be such as can enhance the significance
of the words to the worshippers;

(3) It must be within the power of those who
sing it.

In this order of church music there is at present
conspicuous need for clear thinking, better adjustment, and then indefatigable preparation of such
music as is deemed fit.

There are, in effect, three primary means of utterance
which have to be considered and adjusted, each in its
due proportion, for edifying. These are: *Speech, Song,
Silence.* Corporate speech—as in the spoken Confession; corporate song or chant—as in the Kyrie, Creed
and at other great moments; and purposeful silences
which can be the most dynamic means of all—on occasion more thrilling than the most thrilling music, more
helpful than the very words that prepared the way for
the silence.

Let us suppose that in practice these three really
have their integral part to contribute at the Communion, under ideal circumstances. Possibly this *may*

not be so ; a service may be rightly desired leaving out one of the three. But let it be our working hypothesis here for the moment that not even the most primitive village congregation does well to be without some singing and some silences to enhance the chiefly spoken word ; and that not even the most ornate choral celebration in the cathedral, with the most glorious music, should deprive its worshippers of the boons of silence and the spoken word each in their fitting places. This seems a reasonable supposition.

Now village A, we will imagine, begins musically at "zero." Yet the benignant parson does well to introduce one appropriate hymn at the helpful moment, in which all present can unite.   The rest of the service gains. Village B is better equipped, having learnt to sing simple responses as fluently as they speak them. So they sing the agreed hymn plus the Kyrie, beautifully and naturally uttered together, to some such simple strain as Merbecke. They do this because they find it more orderly, more unanimous and more inspiring than the mixed spoken effort. And here at once is opened up the whole avenue of musical advance along which we may find true congregational song travelling. At villages C, D, E, more and more becomes possible ; gradually it becomes practicable for all to join with heart and soul and perfect decorum in all the greatest moments of utterance in the service, and even to sing back the two boundless replies to the celebrant's "Lift up your hearts" and "Let us give thanks unto our Lord God," at that wonderful moment of the Service.

Of Merbecke's unique pioneer work (under Cranmer's direction) in this regard we shall needs have much to say. He showed the way. He opened up the natural avenue of advance where congregations can ultimately rise to a form of sung worship more thrillingly inspiring to all taking part than is generally realized, and this as naturally as in spoken worship.

But before we consider the possibilities and obligations which Merbecke opened up, let us take a momentary leap beyond all village attainments and imagine the attainments of cathedral A or parish church A where the musical equipment is at its best, and the devotion no less irreproachable. What are the proportions of music, speech and silence there, say, on Easter Day at choral celebration? Our three first conditions named above still apply: (1) The music made there also is acceptable, natural, intelligible; (2) it reverently enhances the service; (3) it is within the powers of those using it. But much of it has now grown so entirely beyond the powers of the congregation that they must for the most part silently co-operate. If they cannot do this it is wrong. Wesley's "Communion Service in E major," for example, answers our three tests nobly so far as choirs are concerned. It is intelligible, eloquent, practicable. But no congregation must try to join in. Hosts of similar settings will occur to readers, all involving the same exclusion of any word from the congregations. Is this exclusiveness wrong? By no means.

The question of absolute right or absolute wrong is at long last beyond any one judgment, or any two, or any committees. Yet we do well to seek diligently here for a clear view of the whole range and in this way for a sane judgment. For these we find pressing need to-day. There is much muddle. A clear view of the field might enable all schools of thought to reach a more refreshing tolerance of each other's thoughts, and to revise and extend their aim. And when this is once attained, though it may be beyond everyone's powers to determine the actual good or the bad of it—*i.e.* of the music here, the spoken word there, the silences here or there—yet it is both urgent and practicable to decide what is fitting or unfitting, what is duly considerate or inconsiderate for worshippers in each time and place.

The *extreme* uses of all three means may possess fitness and show due consideration for extreme needs. But the all-silence extreme, the all-musical extreme, the all-spoken extreme are each of them in turn unlikely to meet the Church's normal needs. In spite of this, there can scarcely be a better preparation for those who are responsible for the adjustment and bettering of our efforts to meet this highest of needs than to experience and ponder over the ideal beauty of these three extremes at their best : (1) The silent service of a Friends' meeting house (we mean the all-silent meeting which, we gather, is now rare); (2) the all-spoken early service at some village church, where the celebrant utters each word with perfect regard for its spiritual intention ; (3) the all-music, say, of Bach's B minor Mass or of Beethoven's Mass in D. To contemplate all three of these experiences (as we do in vivid retrospect at this moment) helps us to attain an unforgettable evaluation of the elemental powers of silence, speech and music.

But this done, the immediate reaction seems to be not towards the adoption of any such extremes, but, instead, towards a fervent conviction that each factor must be given its place everywhere. All-silence is glorious; but it can soon prove too inarticulate for Mr. Smith or Mrs. Jones in their humble service. All-speech is direct, companionable, straightforward; but it can be inadequate for a congregation that could naturally rise to song when song is needed. All-music is admittedly capable of dissolving the poet Milton and others into ecstasies that "bring all heaven before their eyes"; but to bring, let us say, Bach's stupendous Sanctus (which, incidentally, took its rise in the Lutheran Church) into any English Church next Sunday would be like offering a farmer a Niagara to irrigate his small holding. When Cranmer and Merbecke, at the inauguration of the Service in the vernacular, sought some "devout and solemn note" for their purpose, the former declared in a letter to the King that they wanted to find music that might "much excitate the hearts" of the worshippers to true devotion. Precisely; is not this still what we most seek to adjust today to the needs and abilities of each of our choirs and congregations, four hundred years after the event? We would urge that any desire to determine a uniform and literal "right or wrong" as to music at the English Communion Service be recognized as out of the question. Equally we would urge the banishment of any criteria based on personal taste. Both are,

we venture to think, impertinent. But what is both
pertinent and urgent is for all schools of thought to
study (as Cranmer and Merbecke sought to study) the
English worshipper's practical and ideal needs and
capacities when worshipping in English, lovingly and
au fond, and not to rate them either too high or too low.
A faithful and courageous facing, on the part of clergy
and choirmasters alike, of the perpetual questions of
fitness and considerateness must bring some drastic
revisions in more directions than one, correcting, improving—we hope out of all knowledge—both the easy-
going unmusical and the complacent musical services.

And we must no longer consent to fall with
vaguely amiable tolerance between too stools. There
is a natural music, a primal "native note," for the
simplest congregations; for fervent speech naturally
tends to sublimate itself into song. There *is* equally a
music for the most skilful choir to contribute to the
whole, for song tends (just as naturally) to elaborate
itself beyond mere chanting of the words that evoke it,
and to grow richly eloquent; and the greater the
emotion behind the words which move us to music,
the more expansive the music tends to become. What,
then, is most needed? Recognition of both these
means and adjustment of them to their true end.
Faithful enthusiastic development of *both* the congregational note and the choir's music, but with a clear
guiding line drawn between them. After that, our
authorities need more carefully to adjust both orders of
musical effort to the particular needs and powers of
each community. Vision and common sense together

can agree to bring this about. At the moment they do not seem to agree well.

Vision contemplating the whole field may see room in every service for the apt contributions of silent intervals, of speech, of simple (people's) song, and of that more eloquent and illuminating music which lies beyond the congregation's vocal powers but not beyond their spiritual needs. But Commonsense demurs at the attempt to give them all place. It sees insuperable obstacles. For example, it reasonably protests against the sudden transfer from spoken to sung words by clergy or choir. We all know how artificial the effect can be when good speaking ceases, a note is sounded, and bad singing begins, to fall back again at a later point into speech. But it does not follow that natural speech and natural song are incapable of naturally merging into and serving one another at fitting moments. Apart from the obvious fact that sincerity in the use of both is the great merger and unifier, our two friends Commonsense and Vision, sitting side by side on any choir committee, really can collaborate to avoid lumpiness and artificial joins in both visionary and practical ways. Even perfect speaking will refuse to join up to perfect singing if no allowance is made for the nature of both *at the join!* Thus the speaking voice lies generally lower than the singing voice, is generally less effortful, more carefree ; and (perhaps most important of all) syllables are seldom, if ever, sustained in speech as they are in song. It must sound artificial, not to say uncommonly foolish—whether speaking or singing— when a reader abruptly changes his style of utterance in these four ways—suddenly raises the pitch, suddenly increases the effort, suddenly betrays anxiety, and suddenly and arbitrarily lengthens every important syllable. The truth is that neither Vision on the one part nor Commonsense on the other find any necessity whatever for either of these four happenings. They can all be removed. Let it but be faithfully tried in a single church diligently for a single year, and we imagine that church would have worked out quite a useful sum and offered a serviceable example to every congregation in the land. Song such as Merbecke attempted to give us arises out of speech as spontaneously as a bud breaks out of its stem, or as the bud itself in due time breaks into full bloom.

Curiously enough, in the midst of this chapter the writer was called away to play the harmonium at a tiny village church for the simplest form of Sunday morning choral Eucharist. The school-teacher sat at his side and directed him to play two voluntaries ; to accompany the Kyrie (Merbecke), the Ascription before and after the Gospel, and two hymns. As one who signed the Report of the Archbishop's Committee (quoted elsewhere in this book) it was a humbling and reproving experience to the present writer to hear how beautifully and naturally the spoken words of the celebrant and the sung words of the village choir could blend with and fulfil each other. Indeed, the spoken words became unconsciously like sung words. For example, this is how the Sursum Corda was spoken :

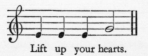

Lift up your hearts.

Speech and song naturally merged and mingled. This does not mean that the Committee's urgent desire to promote unity and consistency of utterance (whether spoken or sung) is not to be followed and even pressed upon those still unmindful of it. It only means that there are far more ways of attaining this end than at least one of the signatories of the Archbishop's Committee's Report had realized. One thing was singularly clear at this restrainedly musical service. The Merbecke melody did fit its purpose astonishingly. It was the "devout and solemn note"; "for every syllable a note"; we took it at a speaking pace yet it proved such as could "excitate the hearts" of this village congregation and choir to devotion; and it was very notable that at the greater moments—especially in the Gloria in Excelsis—the merely spoken word was quite inadequate. It failed completely to "excitate" the singers to devotion. They became listless enough to look this way and that, and not even keep together as they said the great words : "we praise, we bless, we worship, we glorify" . . . it all was positively *belied*, in casual, inadequate speech. Was this the choir's fault? The rector and choirmaster received the suggestion that the preparation of the Gloria should be their next task, with manifest gladness. And this brings us to dwell upon the Merbecke which seems to answer to and fulfil our needs more completely than any service so far made available to villages, towns and cathedral cities alike.

We are unwillingly constrained to speak critically of the present confused views both of the nature and the fitting use of Merbecke's music, in the hope of hastening a happier understanding of both. But first let us try to catch sight of the ideals which are at the back of Merbecke's work and which seemed to have animated all he wrote and given it its lasting practical and exemplary value.

Our readers will have realized that it is precisely when corporate speech grows in unanimity that it nourishes itself into more volume, more orderliness, more contagious oneness, and so tends to merge into something very like primitive melody. Cranmer and Merbecke had prescience to recognize that what happens in unpremeditated song and primitive, melodic impulse was likely to be an important factor in their premeditated supply of notes for the moving moments in vernacular worship. And they obviously knew that not only short ejaculatory people's utterances—such as "Hallelujah!" "Hosanna!" "Kyrie!" or, in the secular field, "Hurrah!"—tended to break into song in the rough, but that *all* fervent words, all words that crystallize emotion, including those that matter deeply to us all, have the same inherent music in them. Merbecke seems quite clearly to have made it his mission to discover and base his "noting" of the English upon this, taken together with, and never ceasing to regard with veneration, the existing church melodies. For, like all intuitive and trusty reformers, he showed profound knowledge of, and reverence for, existing melodies and their uses. He held them within his mind. The old were present with him as he formed the new—or one may almost say as the new formed themselves out of and around the old through his formative mind. A study of the first liturgical melodies in the "Booke of

Common Praier Noted"* (1550) together with the corresponding plainsongs in the older Latin services seems
to reveal more and more close likenesses and reverently
adroit adaptations of the old to the needs of the new.
Never, would it seem, did a "disciple of the Kingdom"
fulfil more than Merbecke the rôle of one who takes
out of his treasure "things new and old." But his task
was, as Cranmer foresaw, to meet the worshipper's need
of direct utterance "in the vulgar tongue," both in
natural speech-rhythms and speech-inflections. There
exist two musical pitfalls in such a case to be avoided.
Melodic elaborateness and all contrapuntal or harmonic
complications are the dangers. Either kind, admirable
in themselves, might fatally tend to obscure the words
as uttered. Only the simplest speech-melody within an
unstrained vocal compass could serve. But within such
severe limits, great and moving eloquence is possible,
provided no musical consideration is allowed to override the paramount verbal needs ; provided, indeed, that
the words are allowed to forge their own melodies spontaneously. One small example from the Creed seems to
speak volumes both as to the actual process and as to
Merbecke's attitude, so manifestly a blend of courageous
reverence for the old and humble search for the new.
Take the following :

Cre - do   in   u - num De - um.

* A good nineteenth-century facsimile reproduction of this,
published by Pickering, can still often be picked up at a reasonable price.

How good it would have been if Merbecke could have retained this venerable strain and set the corresponding six English syllables to the age-old seven-note melody of the seven Latin syllables:

I be-lieve in one God.

But this is not fitting; two notes to the word "God" seem neither natural nor supportable. For it is nowhere the custom of reverent English speech thus to elongate the strong, short, incisive word *God*. So this is truer to the needs of the case:

I be-lieve in one God.

But again this makes "too much of a song" on the little word *in*. We find in the sequel that Merbecke actually gives this word no notes of its own at all, but goes straight to the penultimate note G for the word "one," and moreover proceeds to double the time-value of the latter word "one" (on G) so that the lesser preposition should do no hurt to its greater companion:

in one God.

That is better. But now we see a serious blemish threatening in the adapted plainsong. Merbecke dare not leave it in its ancient form. The two first notes are splendid to the Latin:

Cre - do.

But to give such prominence to the first personal pronoun in the English translation "I believe" is obviously as wrong as the prominent fling of the melody on the first syllable of the word *credo* was right! Merbecke sensitively and stout-heartedly took this in hand. Two versions are to be found. In both the first two notes have given place to low-lying notes:

I   be - lieve   in   one   God.

and:

I   be - lieve   in   one   God.

Both duly place the "I" of the believer on a low note from which the phrase grows upward. And it is not hard to see how aptly both seem now to place every single word of the humble disciple's profession of faith. The rising phrase is a new creation, but still anchored to the old on the crucial words: One God —Deum.

There is perhaps no more typical example of this natural process of forging speech-melody for inspiring congregational purposes than the following Merbecke fragment:

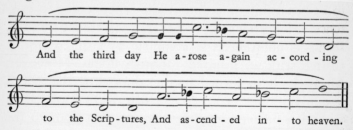

And the third day He a-rose a-gain ac-cord-ing
to the Scrip-tures, And as-cend-ed in-to heaven.

Notice the all-important speech-rhythms of the words "arose again" and "ascended." It is strange, indeed, that Merbecke failed us at the supremely fitting point for song in this service. After the Comfortable Words, the Sursum Corda seems to call out for melodic utterance. Merbecke gives nothing but a monotone speech-rhythm on C, thus:

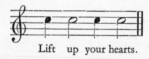

Lift up your hearts.

An increasing number of devout worshippers find it most helpful (as indeed is recommended by the Archbishop's Committee) to substitute the traditional plainsong of the Latin Mass (Sarum use) and this in all cases, syllable by syllable:

Sur - sum cor - da.
Lift up your hearts.

The present writer sees in Merbecke's speech-rhythm above, and in the hundred odd pages of his liturgical music, a clear preclusion of this gentle and moving Latin song from the Merbecke music. It can be imagined to fit beautifully into almost any other setting in existence. To introduce it, however, in Merbecke's works, seems as unfitting as to complete an inspired Gothic church with an inspired Moorish dome. Moreover, Merbecke here opened another door altogether which should faithfully be kept open. Is it, we may ask, either Christian or even intelligent to bar that door to the hundred and more beautiful inflections that sincere utterance of these wonderful words in English may readily reveal and that can crystallize into melodic form highly suited to congregational use? Is this devout "native note" to be rightly suppressed at this of all points, in this of all services? We are constrained, rather, to believe that Merbecke here challenges his followers to note his speech-rhythm and build upon it as humbly and courageously as he built upon his predecessors' work in his far lonelier pioneer work.

Congregational Communion, then, must ever tend to natural, orderly, fervently unanimous delivery of the words appointed to be uttered, whether in speech at quieter moments as in the Confession or in song at the thrilling moments such as the Sursum Corda. Merbecke's was no exclusive solution. It leaves room for every effort both like and unlike itself; itself is the type of many possible solutions.

Other writers in his own day seem to have written on similar lines settings of liturgical parts. Kindred efforts are being made anew today. We are glad to be able to refer to the large and steadily growing supply of music for the Holy Communion fitted more and more admirably for use wherever there is a capable choir and a singing congregation. The choir part is usually in simple polyphony, often modal in flavour, and designed to be sung without organ. There is often no setting of the Creed, nor, in some instances, of the Gloria, the implication being that for these portions Merbecke or plainsong may be sung by choir and congregation. The brevity of the parts allotted to the choir enables the Office to be sung in reasonable time—an important point in churches where Mattins is also sung—and the simple and ecclesiastical character of the set portions minimizes the risk of display in the choir, or distraction or estrangement in the nave. On the congregational side such a service might be made still better by the occasional use of other music than Merbecke for the Creed. The tuneful "Missa de Angelis" might well be drawn on. It is more elaborate than the twelfth-century plainsong Creed now widely used; but it is also easier, and likely to be well taken up in quarters where the severity of the older plainsong might be a hindrance.

We would here offer a warning against the ever-threatening risk of musical over-elaborateness. Euphony is beguiling in itself. But the musician at worship must remain at all points the servant of the people at worship with him. We must refrain from elaborating either melody or harmony beyond the people's mind to accept or follow. There is for example an adapted Easter plainsong revived in the "English Hymnal" (presumably for use) in which more than

twenty notes are set to be sung to the second syllable
of the word "Passover." This may have been the
sincere melodic expression of rapturous devotion by
men long ago to whom twenty notes in this connection
were more joyously natural than one. But a lovable
ancient church tradition is not of necessity either the
natural or practicable or even adaptable vehicle of an
English congregation at worship today. Our link with
the revered past must be something more vitally akin
than this. Similarly elaborate harmonies of Victorian
days, and descants (of various size, compass and age),
can be devout to the musical enthusiast and devastating
to his congregation.

This brings us to closer grips with the choir's and the
organist's true function, at Holy Communion especially,
but in other parts of the service also. Taking organist
and choir together as the potential expert helpers and
leaders of the people, fortifiers and illuminators of the
congregational melody, they can obviously be used
in two ways simultaneously—for the one part doubling
the congregation's melody, and for the other part fitly
adorning it with added harmonies or added melodies;
these neither obscuring nor detracting from the chief
song, but supporting and enhancing it. That added harmonies and added melodies can naturally and helpfully
function in this way is unquestionable. Let the simplest
examples be recalled. Here is a truly congregational
phrase from the well-known tune "Nicæa" to Heber's
words:

Ho - ly,   Ho - ly,   Ho - ly!

How three strong diapason chords on the organ can strengthen and enrich it is familiar to all. For a homely melodic example, we have only to remember our fathers' habit of enriching a tune by extemporizing thirds and sixths there and then in the congregation—a device which, fifty years ago, was called "singing seconds." The present writer can remember the zest with which he looked forward to a tune which went as follows:

because he knew that if he stood on the seat with his ear close to his mother's face, she would make the tune uniquely enjoyable by adding thirds:

Descants are a manifestation of this intuition to amplify, without confusion, the people's part. But through all this, especially when half the choir sings with the people and the other half supplies complete harmonic accompaniment, it is imperative that the tendency to hold up the rhythm and harmonically stereotype it should be resisted. It is interesting to note how early harmonic enrichment of the people's melody occurred in the lovely Lord's Prayer, by Merbecke's contemporary, Stone, recently made available in its original form by Mr. C. F. Simkins.* Such speech-harmonies, as they may be called, should be sung in the same natural shorts and longs as the people's part. It seems strange that the custom has grown up of accompanying with organ harmonies to the exclusion of choral accompaniment. A moment's thought and a week's experience will convince anyone how serviceable it is to reverse this custom and use the organ (as it undoubtedly was used of old) to support the people's part, leaving supporting harmonies to such of the choir as can be spared for the purpose.

A tactful distribution of accompaniment and support would seem to be best attainable by some such plan as the following:

1. *Main Portion of Choir.*—To sing with the people in the simplest speech-melody of the Merbecke type.
2. *Select Portion of Choir.*—To sing accompanying "speech-harmonies" in the most melodious ways available.
3. *Organ.*—To play the chief melody in support of the people, occasionally supporting the select portion of choir with their added accompaniments.

The organ must play speakingly and so meet the congregation who speak singingly.

* S.P.C.K.

Only a word or two need be added at this point as to
the more formal musical settings used by many churches
at the Communion, since they stand in reality in the
same category as the voluntary settings and larger
musical offerings discussed in Chapter XIII., where the
nature and requirements of such settings are fully considered. What is said there applies with even greater
urgency here. All musical glories must be utterly considerate of the people's needs. Their welfare is the
supreme concern of every note of music sung. That
means that their silent participation must be realized;
indeed, it should be made as easy to hear and take part in
as to speak or sing and take part in the very worship
itself.

And now we must turn once more from general considerations to offer such criticisms and suggestions as
we are able on the situation today in regard to the
present use and abuse of Merbecke. In his setting the
English Church has something that might have long ago
become a priceless possession, *i.e.* a setting of the Communion Office that could be joined in, with confidence,
by all church folk, in parish church and cathedral alike.
But the opportunity has not been fully used, owing to
a variety of causes. At the time of writing there are
fifteen editions! All differ in some respects from one
another, and some from the original, in the method
of setting forth; in one passage, "sitteth at the right
hand of the Father," the melody has been altered
for reasons that seem to us to be insufficient (the
more so as the original is both superior on musical
grounds and had become familiar to congregations

before the change was made); there are two schools of thought concerning the method of performance, one maintaining that the music is plainsong and should be notated and rendered as such: the other holding that, as Merbecke used notes of varying lengths (the relative values of which he plainly set forth in a preface) the music belongs rather to the measured type, to be sung freely, yet with musical as well as verbal rhythm ; and there is similar divergence of view as to harmonization, the plainsong party claiming that the music is modal, the other side seeing in the setting a mixture of modal and modern tonality most fittingly harmonized in the style of Merbecke's day. After careful consideration of all the arguments, it seems to us that Merbecke's setting is, as Dr. Colles says in "Grove," "neither plainsong in the technical sense (notes of undefined value) nor mensural music (notes of strict value) but a typically English compromise between the two." Merbecke's accentuation and his indications of speech-rhythms in note-values are adversely criticized by those who, in ignorance of the true nature of music itself, take them fixedly. When Parry set Milton's line, "O may we soon again renew that song," using, like Merbecke, three values of notes, he indicated lengths on the first and fourth syllables and shortness on the fifth, and this much in Merbecke's manner :

Sing in stock-values, and you violate both Milton's
and Parry's inspiration; but do not adversely criticize
Parry if you fail to understand that quavers that grow
on musical branches can no more be sung to stock size
than leaves on nature's branches can be found to be
ever exactly alike. Merbecke has been plentifully abused
recently. Let his light-hearted critics abuse Parry, who
also was a devout speech-rhythm composer and not
impeccable. Let them do more for their own good
and treat Parry as they have treated Merbecke:

O may we soon a - gain re - new that song.

in order, forsooth, to help choirs to truer English-
inspired speech-values than Parry's well-meant markings, and they will reflect: is even mensural music
ever fully written to the eye? Is music as free as
branches in nature, and never made to measure? What,
then, were Parry and Merbecke most keen to do? To
help their singers by a few careful pattern-suggestions
to unify their utterance without loss of freedom? Are
the equal notes of plainsong notation meant to hamper
that very freedom? With such thoughts in mind, we
would beseech our plainsinging friends to reconsider
the whole position again and again, as we have done
and intend to do, with larger conceptions of the true
nature of song, plain or adorned, of music mensural or
non-mensural.

Regarded as a bridge between, and combination of,

ancient and modern methods of setting a prose text, and sung accordingly, Merbecke's service is, we feel, of greater historical interest and far more effective than either the strict plainsong version on the one hand, or the modernized Stainer edition on the other.

An exemplary congregational setting of the Communion Service that would set the standard is an ideal that the church has not yet achieved, owing to this disturbing variety of editions. Is it too late to do what ought to have been done a few decades ago? The Roman Church is setting the example in trying to arrive at an agreed form of the Ordinary of the Mass; cannot the English Church arrive at an agreed Merbecke? A representative body of clerical scholars and practical musicians could surely be relied on to meet this need. Publication difficulties ought not to be allowed to stand in the way. They could perhaps be overcome by the simple expedient of throwing open the rights of publication, a proportion of the proceeds of sales being devoted to a number of church music causes that will command general approval, *e.g.* the School of English Church Music, the Plainsong and Mediæval Music Society, and the Organists' Benevolent League. The editions should include some that may be bound up in the most widely used sizes of prayer-books.

To conclude: what should be our attitude musically to the Divine Office, and, in it, towards each other, musicians and congregation alike? The musician must not suffer surprise if so profound a service move him to attempt the impossible, *i.e.* a music so full, so musical (compared with the spoken word that actually evoked his music), so elaborate as to be unacceptable to the ordinary worshippers. And worshippers should, for their part, regard tolerantly and gratefully the musician, if great words move him to expansive music. But both must give and take in agreement. Only the most perfect music perfectly rendered is just good enough for the humblest worshipper at this of all services. We must ruthlessly cut out everything in the nature of display. All must be subject to the occasion and the spirit of it. Congregations for their part can frankly accept sincere music, taking part silently as they do in the sincere reading or singing of a great prayer when one alone is uttering but all are praying. This is only really hard to do when shortcomings (on one side or on both) make it so. Let us musicians for our part revere the sublime attainments of Bach's B minor and Beethoven's Solemn Mass in D. Yet let our music at the Communion be in all ways as simple as it can and only as elaborate as it must. Simple or elaborate, let our care for and practice of it be never-ending : for it is certain that in this mystic Service above all others, when we have done our utmost we shall most vividly know ourselves to be unprofitable servants.

CHAPTER XIII

CANTICLE SETTINGS, ANTHEMS AND OTHER VOLUNTARY MUSIC

THE word "voluntary" in the caption serves as a reminder that anthems and settings of the canticles are not obligatory, save in cathedrals and collegiate churches. Their use elsewhere, however, is admissible, and may be desirable, provided again that certain simple conditions, like those already noted in other connections, be observed: (1) The introduction of such voluntary music and the frequency of its use should have due regard to the traditions—both musical and otherwise—of the church, and to the needs and desires of the congregation as a whole; (2) the examples chosen must be of good quality both as music and as church music; (3) they must be well within the capabilities of the choir.

The first of these conditions raises again points of vital importance on the human side. For musical issues musicianship is needed, but for human issues clergy, choir and choirmaster need only be thoroughly human; and we can all see that if at any point the musical and humane are momentarily at variance, the latter must be given first consideration. It is one of the choirmaster's responsibilities to see that they are reconcilable.

"I like So-and-So's anthems," said one of our greatest living bishops, "because there are always plenty of words to them." It is inhuman to ask a bishop, to whom ideas are very life itself, to spend five minutes over an idea which engaged his mind for half a minute at most, and therefore leaves him for nine out of ten minutes healthily impatient to get on. The anthems he liked gave him clues, something to ponder in known words which unknown music expounded.

Most readers will know of the famous dean who, having a copy of the anthem always placed in his stall, exclaimed to a friend: "I look at the price, and when it is three-halfpence, I know I'm all right; but when I see 'price sixpence,' I tremble!" Was this a lack of education in the dean, or of the humane touch in the music, or both? When we say "lack of education" here, we mean many things, many aspects of education. Least of all do we mean education in purely musical questions. From infancy that dean's *eye* had been trained both by use and teaching, and also by deliberate exercise, to detect and enjoy visible beauty in objects of every kind, whether in nature or in art and handiwork around him, and also to detect and abhor ugliness and shortcoming. But what "Eton and Balliol" dean, or, indeed, what literary genius, soldier or statesman can say that from infancy his *ear* had been exercised and taught (self-taught or otherwise) to detect and admire audible beauty and to detect and abhor audible ugliness? All this will, doubtless, be changed some day; and a chapter on anthems in a book on church music fifty years on will be at no pains to put this point we now are endeavouring to make clear. Yet we suspect that in every such book, for ages yet, choirs and composers alike will still need to be exhorted to be sensible enough to consider and meet the needs of worshippers, from the bishop to the humblest member of the congregation.

Yet another reminiscence may help us here. We once heard an eminent cabinet minister excitedly commend an anthem he had just heard. He did it with the air of a man who had made a sudden discovery. "It was all so exciting!" he exclaimed enthusiastically; "there was the cry of a soul in trouble, getting no answer to prayer; then you heard the enemy overwhelming him, and the greater cry and horror; then the music gave us the utter loneliness of blank despair, and at last the picture of rest." Such were his ideas. The reader may have guessed that the anthem was the overworked and sometimes musically despised Mendelssohn's "Hear my Prayer."

From these three typical instances we may deduce a useful fact or two about all our efforts at illumination and exposition of spiritual experiences in terms of music, *i.e.* in anthems, elaborate settings of canticles, cantatas, voluntaries—in short, in all voluntary church music. The bishop asked for words; the dean required brevity;* the statesman's need was the human touch. To all three, and to three million other such men today, most music is at present what St. Paul calls a "tongue." They had rather hear five notes sung with understanding than ten thousand in a tongue. But then—five notes sung are gone in a second or so. How are they to be remem-

---

* Incidentally, of course, it is to be remembered that "price 1½d." often means a well-known classic, and the Dean's tastes may have been Handelian.

bered? Imagine that five words appeared in a motto or inscription at the east end of every church (say, at anthem time) for one moment, and then disappeared from sight; would the bishop, dean, statesman and everybody else get good hold of it, and be grateful? This brings us to the vexed question of musical repetition of words in anthems. Our critics will realize that there is such a thing as anthem architecture that accounts for verbal repetitions. They do not call pillar upon pillar, arch upon arch of their favourite cathedral "vain repetition"; nor do they laugh at such a feature. When they cultivate an eye for church architecture they should try to cultivate an ear for musical architecture too. This is not asking a hard thing. It is not harder to acquire the hearing ear than the seeing eye, but the latter is rarely given the consideration that is its due.

Having said this, we are free to admit the absurdities and complacencies of the repetitions in foolish anthems. There is, for example, a notorious work called "Ruth" in which many pages of loud chorus are devoted to repetitions of the words "and his name was Boaz," to say nothing of other astonishing examples of an unbelievable convention. However, this is not the place to enter into the problems of words and music which face us today. Absurdities are still rife in almost every vocal field. But we can perhaps usefully summarize the needs and just desires of our congregations in regard to all set music at services. We must ask them to respond to Beauty made audible as they would to Beauty made visible in God's House. But that being said, we must take care to give them the real article, both in composition and in rendering. And the ideas underlying the anthem must not be an enigma, vaguely expounded musically. The bishop asked for plenty of words, but he really required *ideas*; abundance of clear thought under the beautiful sounds. If Nature abhors a vacuum, our higher nature, our creative mind, must needs abhor it still more. This is the lesson of "Hear my Prayer." Mendelssohn made no secret of the manly ideas behind it all. Better, fitter music will succeed it. Men will stand on Mendelssohn's shoulders and benefit by his faithful genius. But they must embody the thoughts and feelings and aspirations of the worshipping Christian *as articulately as he did* ; and the more mystically beautiful church music becomes, the greater its obligations to be articulate. Wesley knew this secret. "The Wilderness" was rejected by musical adjudicators. But it is a human document, a vivid new thing, a spiritual music, though with plenty of musical defects, which even a pedestrian doctor of music can detect. It survives these defects. And on simpler lines, such an anthem as the old "Lord, for Thy tender mercies' sake" (especially with the beautiful final Amens of the more recent Church Music Society's edition*) fulfils the same needs, demands and desires of all men, if perfectly sung. Of the work of living writers, it may not be invidious to single out two as examples of elaborate and modern anthems which yet fulfil the common needs described. In "Lord, Thou hast been our refuge,"† Vaughan Williams has broken new ground. Not the slowest

* Oxford University Press.   † Messrs. Curwen.

imagination can fail to be quickened by the alternation (for double choir) of the serene Christian hymn, to its familiar St. Anne, sung by one choir in a whisper, with the sublimely dark Jewish pathos of the original psalm, chanted by the opposite choir in a kind of despairing recitative ; and the final merging of both Jewish and Christian utterance into a prayer that the God of all would "prosper the handiwork" of all. Nor can the plain man, if responsively inclined, miss the seven imaginative facets of a well-known hymn, "O quanta qualia," which Dr. W. H. Harris has given to the seven stanzas in his anthem, "O what their joy and their glory must be."* But now we must turn to the question of local traditions.

There are churches where entirely congregational music is a tradition : at others canticle settings are customary, but anthems taboo ; at yet other churches, plainsong is used for psalms and canticles, and anthems sung only very rarely. The proportion of settings or anthems in any of these circumstances should, in our judgment, neither be increased or lessened without careful consideration. The musical traditions of a church, especially when those traditions make for a congregational type of service, are often a strong unifying element, not to be hazarded, but preserved. True, their preservation may raise a problem, for a skilful choir often finds in the simple round of services a lack of outlet for its zeal and ability. A good solution is the occasional performance of extra-liturgical music. In the shape of monthly, or less frequent, recitals of

* Oxford University Press.

choral and organ music (preferably after the evening service, which may well be slightly shortened for the occasion), this is being done increasingly in churches and chapels where exist the apparently incongruous elements of a simple service and a first-rate choir. The recital may be of short works of the anthem type, a cantata, a seasonable portion of "The Messiah"— there is hardly a limit to the field of choice. In places where good amateur instrumentalists are available all sorts of possibilities soon reveal themselves. We know a suburban Wesleyan church where there are monthly recitals, the programmes ranging from Elizabethan motets to a Bach cantata, from an "Elijah" selection to a substantial choral work by Parry. Better far this occasional music-making, which members of the congregation may choose or not to attend, than weekly anthems and settings for which, owing to long custom, the real and general desire has still to be quickened.

Our second condition given at the outset of this chapter brings up once more the question of taste. There is a lot of muddled thinking on this point, many people having made up their mind (apparently without first using it) that a piece of music is just a piece of music, and so something to like or dislike, but impossible to classify as good or bad.

A little reflection will show that there is in the whole of music a vast range of works of every conceivable style—including dance music—concerning whose excellence there has long been agreement among musicians. A similar state of things exists in every art, of course ;

yet many a normal person of good education who can readily distinguish between good and bad work in literature and the fine arts becomes vague concerning musical standards. It must be remembered that books and pictures, sculpture and architecture, are sufficiently related to real life to enable him to recognize, and to be influenced by, the more obvious technical virtues and defects. No mere colour-scheme, however pleasing, will reconcile him to, *e.g.*, a piece of ludicrously bad perspective. With music he is on a far less assured footing, being conscious only of what sounds pleasing. Appreciation of a composer's craft is beyond him : he is not easily persuaded that music, to be indisputably good, must comprise among its elements certain important factors of which only the musicians are aware. A clumsy bass, a bad "join," poor part-writing, weak "lay-out" of harmony : to the expert ear these are what the false perspective and incompetent drawing are to the eye of the intelligent non-musician. It has to be said frankly that, to be of value, an opinion on musical quality must be based on musical understanding and a considerable degree of familiarity with the corpus of music in common use. As with the general, so with the particular ; and anyone with an all-round knowledge of the church music repertory will find little difficulty in choice, so far as quality is concerned.

Contrary to popular opinion, then, the question of good and bad quality in music is not one of mere taste, nor even of agreed fitness only, but of standards of good workmanship discernible and generally accepted by those qualified by knowledge to give advice. Taste is personal, and the fact that it often leads to a deliberate choice of the bad no more damages the case for a standard of quality in art than deliberate misconduct weakens the case for a standard in morals. It is astonishing that today, after more than a decade of broadcasting, with all its opportunities of self-education in such matters, there are still intelligent people who think they can dispose of a question of musical choice, whether it be of a wireless programme or of a piece of church music, by a mere assertion that they "know what they like." Incalculable harm has been done to the cause of church music by the toleration—even respect—with which this attitude has been viewed by both clerical and musical authorities. Of all the signs of weakness in direction none is worse than that implied in the remark, "We must give the people what they like." But who are "they"? In what way have "their" likings been ascertained? And why is it so often assumed that the liking will be for music of various degrees of badness? In even a small congregation there will be found markedly different tastes and degrees of musical knowledge. Some folk have an instinctive appreciation for the good in music, as others have in dress, furniture, food, etc.; and to these have now to be added the growing number whose musical perceptions are in a constant state of development through the agency of broadcasting. (The fact that this development is often unconscious makes it none the less real.) The time is rapidly approaching—if, indeed, it is not already here—when to give a congregation the music it likes will be to give it nothing but good.

The second half of our second proviso must not be forgotten : the music must be good *church* music. The principle is best put logically : All fitting music is good, but not all good music is fitting.

In regard to both quality and fitness there will always be a proportion of music that is on the border line ; and (especially so far as style is concerned) most of these debatable examples will be found to belong to periods of decline in music generally, or in church music in particular, or even in church life itself. More than once the decline in church music has coincided with the advance in secular music—has even been due to that advance. For example, the Haydn-Mozart-Beethoven period was one of the greatest in the history of music so far as development of the art and its resources was concerned ; but it was one of the worst for church music, partly for that very reason. As there was no corresponding growth on the lines of the two great polyphonic schools that reached their culmination in Palestrina and Bach, church music became submerged, and the difference between music for the church and that for the opera and the concert-room became almost negligible. A similar state of things is seen in English church music of the Restoration period. The chief developments were in the direction of harmony, instrumental forms, and music for stage purposes. (The low condition of the devotional life of the church itself was also a factor.) That is why the greatest natural genius in English music, though organist of Westminster Abbey, wrote comparatively little church music that can be used today without some allowance being made for the period and circumstance of its origin.

This question of "making allowance" is one of considerable importance ; it means a temporary adjustment of the listener's views and tastes, and without it a great deal of fine music that has become of doubtful fitness through the passing of time and changes of taste could never be heard. That this adjustment is not to be sweepingly condemned as a mere temporizing with inferiority may be shown by many instances, of which we choose one of the most familiar—Purcell's "Rejoice in the Lord." Judged by present-day standards of what is ecclesiastically fit, it may be condemned. Yet its naively cheerful strains and secular rhythms may be helpfully sung and heard not only by "naively cheerful" people, but by all those who are able to appreciate its sincerity and to "tune in" to the composer and his time.

We have been somewhat discursive on this question of quality and fitness, because we are convinced that much of the confusion of mind that exists amongst clergy, organists and congregation alike is due not to lack of the necessary large-mindedness so much as to a lack of the historical sense. In the Preface to "A History of Music,"* Professor Buck says :

> " . . . the history of a thing—music or anything else—seems to me to be not only the most interesting part of it, but also the one part that must be known before the thing can be under-

* Benn's Sixpenny Library.

stood. Yet of the millions of music lovers in the world, but one here and there has ever even dipped into a history of music."

To many this will be a hard saying. Perhaps only a minority will share Professor Buck's feeling that the history of a thing is the most interesting part of it. But nobody can, after reflection, deny that to understand anything we are in a better position the moment we know its history, and there can be no real church musicianship without power to grasp the glory of all schools and periods. These matter more than names, because all great composers possess the power to feel forward and backward. Even such a man as Boyce, for instance, can show three styles in a single anthem. Thus, his "Turn thee unto me" opens with nobly emotional polyphony that might have come from the greatest of the Elizabethans ; the second movement is a treble duet in the tuneful, homely, even complacent style of Boyce's own day ; the third is a florid fugato suggestive of very good Handel. The study of musical history is full of such examples of the slow merging of school into school. The Boyce anthem remains a fine work despite its seeming confusion of styles ; the large mind will hear its unity ; and to those with a sense of history the confusion is not a defect, but a point of great interest.

Having embarked on this historical digression, let us carry it a degree farther, and pause to point out how throughout the ages English church music has its unifying points of contact. Of many, let us take one easily verifiable example. Here is the last line of the

Sarum form of the hymn-tune "Veni creator spiritus":*

Observe the beautiful suavity of the flat—music's first accidental : it was an early convention (with a common-sense vocal reason) that when the B lay between two A's, it should usually be flattened. Now see Tallis, centuries after this hymn-tune was written, using the progression harmonically, with added beauty brought about by the juxtaposition of flat and natural :

And here, from a multitude of examples of the period, is Gibbons's version, stronger, as befits the text, "Hosanna to the Son of David" :

* For ease of comparison all the examples appear in the same key.

Purcell's constant employment of the device left it unexhausted, and we find Samuel Sebastian Wesley, in his evening service in E, playing with it for a page or two thus :

The progression has been maintained with very few breaks throughout the story of English music, especially English church music (the rarity of its use by the later Victorian school was probably due to the strong element of false relationship), though Wesley made, perhaps, the most poignantly developed use of it on record in his anthem "Man that is born of a woman" ; it has been treated in a variety of ways (the Elizabethans and Purcell did not scruple on occasion to sound both flat and natural together !) and our living composers of church music still find good use for it. The devotional power of that B flat has been everywhere recognized. Organists will recall an exquisite instance at the double bar in Bach's "Schmücke dich" ; and in the "Et resurrexit" of Beethoven's "Missa Solemnis" it appears with electrifying effect.

All this shows, we hope, that the study of musical history and style can be of great interest ; and its practical value soon becomes apparent to those who take seriously their responsibility as choosers and inter-preters of the church's music.

The third proviso concerning the use of non-obligatory music is that it should be well within the capabilities of the singers.* This needs emphasizing rather than pointing out, and the emphasis should be on what we will call the two-fold margin of (1) safety and (2) interpretative scope. The first is rarely wide enough, because church choirs, like amateur dramatic societies, are apt to grudge that last little bit of work, that final pinch of pains, the importance of which per-haps few but professionals realize fully. Only to amateurs is vouchsafed the optimism that in the face of a dozen shaky leads and untidy ensembles, can express itself in the typically English and happy-go-lucky phrase, "It'll be all right on the night!"

The standard of church choir singing would go up at a bound if, say, a hundred choirs, scattered about the country, suddenly became zealots, smitten with a passion for perfection. No longer would they be con-tent with first performances that are virtually final re-hearsals; their zeal would express itself in a new slogan, even breaking out into a rough rhyme : "It *shall* be all right On the last practice night."

The margin for interpretation starts at this point. The excellence of that first singing will inevitably be mainly of the letter; every subsequent practice and rendering will reveal more and more of the spirit, until

* The accompaniment of much modern church music is so difficult and independent that the capabilities of the organist and the resources of his instrument have also to be considered.

real interpretation is achieved. If it be argued that both zeal and standard alike are unattainable by church choirs, we ask objectors to explain away the fact that town and village choral societies of men, women, and children of exactly the same type as those in church and chapel choirs (many, in fact, are members of those choirs) can in competition festivals reach and sometimes pass the 90 per cent. mark, often in music making more demands than that which the church choirs of the same calibre would be called on to sing in church. We know all that can be said in reply—that the competition choir has only a few songs to study, and can spend many months on them; that the stimulus of competition helps them; and so on. But a very large proportion of the church-choir repertory consists of familiar and very simple things, the amount of new music to be studied depending on the time and energy the choir is prepared to give; and as for stimulus, ought church choirs to need any more than that provided by the honour and privilege of their position?

Happily, there do exist church choirs whose aim at the best is constant. They may be heard in village and town alike; and they belong to no particular parts of the country. Being situate in Wales or Yorkshire has little to do with the matter—"little" rather than "nothing," because the Celt brings to choral singing temperament, and the Yorkshireman vocal energy, to a degree not usual in other parts of the country; but the things that count are the aim and the effect. So you may hear very bad choirs as well as good in Wales and Yorkshire; and *vice versa* in East Anglia, Wessex, the

Midlands—anywhere, in fact, and sometimes in the oddest and most surprising corners. But one thing is significantly certain : whatever the vocal resources may be, you will never find a bad choir where there is a good choirmaster, so the moral is plain.

Here, then, is the position of the choir and choral musician generally towards anthems and all other voluntary music. The obligation is not in the undertaking. They are free to undertake anthems or not ; but this very freedom of action defines their obligation that the choice shall be fitting and the singing worthy.

Instead of giving lists of suitable music, we have preferred to consider the general principles by which choice should be governed. Lists, after all, say little or nothing on some crucial points, nor can there be finality about such guides ; good new works, such as those referred to earlier in the chapter, appear constantly, together with reprints and improved editions of old ones. The choirmaster should choose for himself, and he can do this easily and safely by taking advantage of the facilities now given by most publishers of choral music. He should (*a*) make out a list of likely works, drawn from catalogues, review columns, etc., and send it to the publisher with a request for specimen copies on approval ; or (*b*) he should write for a selection of works of a specified style and degree of difficulty, also on approval. In the latter case it is well to mention a few familiar things well within the powers of his choir. (If the choir is very large or very small, or unusual in balance or in any other respect, the fact should be mentioned.) The sample copies can usually be retained for a fortnight, no charge being made if the copies are returned in due time.

Other helps are to be found in the review columns of musical journals, which give fairly full details as to character, degree of difficulty, etc. Not least among the advantages of affiliation to the School of English Church Music are the descriptive and classified lists of parish church music, new and old, that appear in the journal issued by the School. We add an expression of regret that the church newspapers now give far less space than formerly to the reviewing of church music.

The title of this chapter suggests that it ought to embrace music played as well as sung, so we end with a brief plea for the organ music that precedes and ends the service—the voluntary. Like the choir's voluntary music, that of the organist must be good, fitting for the place and the occasion, and worthily performed. With an improved standard in these respects will certainly come a more responsive and appreciative attitude on the part of the congregation.

The size of the organ and the skill of the player matter less than is generally supposed : tasteful playing of quite simple (but good) music will often hold a congregation whose departure might be quickened by the complex or flamboyant. Organ music before the service should consist of a set piece or pieces unless the player is a gifted or at least coherent improviser. Good timing is necessary. An advantage of the use of set pieces for in-voluntaries is that it keeps in circulation, so to speak, much beautiful and suitable music that is too quiet or meditative for playing at other times. Now that so much first-rate organ music is broadcast, and the general public is becoming acquainted with the repertory, the out-voluntaries ought to be included in the music list. (We know of some churches where the in-voluntary is given as well.) The voluntary, both in and out, may now be made relevant to the service, thanks to the wealth of organ music, old and new, based on ecclesiastical themes. Where instrument and opportunity allow of frequent recitals, the distinction between voluntaries and concert pieces should be more clearly made than is usually the case. The organ repertory is far larger, better in quality, and richer in scope, than is generally realized. Recital programmes consisting mainly of choral preludes and other music more suitable for use in connection with a service give the public a totally wrong impression of the instrument and its resources. A recital, even in a church, belongs to the concert genus, and while suited in aspiration and dignity to its environment should yet be as varied, skilful and attractive as any other form of solo recital. It has even more incentive to be masterly.

CHAPTER XIV

DIOCESAN AND OTHER FESTIVALS

FOR many years it has been clear that there is not a village church in the country which could not have its Church Choral Union. This has been abundantly proved, as already suggested, by the Competitive Festival Movement, where the standard attained by the village choral societies, in part-song, madrigal and cantata, has been astonishing. The country only awaits its musical *staffing*. When anything remarkable has been done by a small village, there is always an indefatigable local enthusiast at the bottom of it all, and with him or her one or more to make a working committee. The squire's thoroughly musical daughter has been trained perhaps at the Royal College of Music, and has caught the festival and conducting infection, very likely at a summer school; and the "Matthew Passion" itself becomes a village possibility.

But we are not quite there yet; for the competitive village or district orchestra is still a rare thing; the village church choirs are generally, and almost totally, incompetent to sing skilled music well enough themselves, and are often an unconscious hindrance to the undertaking because they have not been called upon to relate themselves to their more musical neighbours the choral and orchestral societies, nor to work together with them at "The Messiah" or the Passion music. A moment's thought will make it clear to all that the primal need is co-operation and the agreed mobilization of all available and willing musical material, not only the existing choirs, the congregation and their friends, but the musical powers of the whole parish. A music committee with organist and choirmaster, all musical enthusiasts, and a presiding chairman and secretary are needed.

Let us suppose that this has been achieved ; and, to fly high, let nothing less than a devout and adequate rendering of the "Matthew Passion" some Friday in Lent be the determined aim of the parish church or chapel in question. With this in mind it may be helpful to review the needs and practical possibilities.

(1) First the glory of the aim of it all must be made clear to all concerned ; without cant or priggishness everyone must consciously agree that personal powers and proclivities are to be merged, in unruffled good humour, into the one great purpose of offering an ideal musical service to the parish. As in the old days the people must "offer themselves willingly" with no nonsense of "I want to sing or play this or that part." This is said here, because, from experience, we have found that failure comes from not having made the vision clear till after the petty personal "taking offence" has begun. Tell the whole "expeditionary force" from the first that they are going to climb a musical Everest, and they are less likely to trouble about their personal comfort on the journey.

(2) Next come the series of friendly committee and unofficial sub-committees—meeting over cups of tea

at each other's houses—in order to outline the actual organization. Who is to be the conductor C.-in-C.? Who are to be his assistants? These may include his chief organist and assistant organist; his assistant chorus-master for the "Congregational Choral Union"; assistant coach for the local instrumental contingent; assistant choirmaster for teaching the boys and men of the regular church choir the chorals; music librarian and registrar of attendances at practices. Now it is easy to foresee that there may be many different successful solutions. This imposing list of seven major jobs might very easily be mastered by two indefatigable and friendly men—the conductor of the Choral Union and the organist of the church—in close collaboration. It might be that three men would do it far better, one of them imported solely for this emprise.

(3) Here comes the practical question: how much professional help will be required? Clearly, the chief solo parts will call for first-class exponents: above all, the exacting rôle of Narrator must be well filled. Singers will usually be willing to consider a reduced fee for local enterprises of the sort we are discussing; and in many cases it may possibly be best for the local enthusiast conducting and the organist to agree that they will invite a professional conductor to take supreme and final command, they themselves undertaking all subsidiary leaderships together. There will probably be among the chorus a few men quite capable of singing the subsidiary solo parts: and the solo and contralto arias may be sung by a section of the boys in unison. The short choruses of disciples could, with

good effect, be allotted to a semi-chorus of men. And so the organizers would continue to carry out their absorbingly interesting task of allocation of parts in domestic conclave.

(4) The first meeting of all who are to take part would perhaps best be held in a parish hall or practice room with a piano. All would have their copies, and the conducting C.-in-C. accepted and appointed formally by all. He would perhaps sketch the whole adventure to those assembled and run through a few points at the piano, or with the help of his accompanist, and the occasion should again be not without a warm social atmosphere.

It should be made clear to all that no limit would be set to the number of practices. These would depend upon progress, and everybody must be prepared to come to as many practices as are needed at all costs to themselves. It is astonishing how heroic choirs can become if they see the point of it all clearly enough to make the effort worth while. Sectional practices have a special value in developing self-reliance.

And here we want to tell a story of the preparation and performance of this very work by town and village choirs in Wales eleven years ago. This particular incident may be helpful to readers who see no way of rising to such a height in their village or town alone, but who do see possible means—perhaps through the Festival Movement itself—of achieving it together with neighbour choirs. About twenty-two choirs in Montgomeryshire agreed in 1923 to prepare the "St.

Matthew Passion" for combined performance at their County Festival. Many were very small villages; and, as time went on, the task of preparation became too discouraging to endure. A conference of conductors met to beg their chief conductor to abandon the project. After discouraging discussions, a ray of light dawned in the C.-in-C.'s mind. He made an appeal to the conductors to meet him again at the same spot two or three weeks hence and each bringing four members of his own choir—delegates of each part. This was done. The "delegate choir" which resulted brought the conference up to some hundred souls. (Not a village but could get its motor to hold five and assemble at any given point at a given time.) This particular assembly met in a valley five miles from a railway station in the music room of a large private house. The singing that day was astonishing and unforgettable to all concerned, and swept all fears before it. The delegates returned inspired to carry the good hopes to their own choirs, and the final performance together was assured. It seems possible that this almost chance happening prefigures a way in which every county in Britain could achieve similar heartening results, and carry the system further. For there is nothing to prevent the "delegate choir" from serving any and every village church or chapel that may desire their help by this neighbourly "form fours" system of making a picked representative choir, forty, sixty, or eighty strong, a "flying column" for service anywhere in the county, diocese or district; provided always, and only, that it be used to help and stimulate, never to usurp or discourage the home team's own efforts. We venture to think it a not too distant dream that all cathedrals and pro-cathedral churches may some day foster their own choral delegate choirs (as a matter of course), drawn from every village which chooses to affiliate with them. In this way, the picked singers of each unit, each year, would find themselves, in their year of office, singing shoulder to shoulder with other picked singers of their own calibre. They would go back to their own people more able to lead, and leaven up the lump. No musical glory would be impossible. The lesser places would be serviceably united to their cathedral centres. The mother churches, daughter churches, sister churches, would all musically realize the "hidden soul of harmony" which makes them one.

Such enterprises have already been carried out magnificently in some English centres. The "St. Matthew Passion" was given at Peterborough Cathedral in 1927, with a chorus of 1,400 drawn from forty centres; there were first-rate soloists, a full professional orchestra; some of the smaller choirs sang the chorales only; the audience numbered 4,000. The moving spirit and conductor was the cathedral organist, Dr. Henry Coleman. And much the same sort of impossible-sounding achievements are brought off successfully at a number of English competition festivals, chiefly in rural districts, where the aim is co-operation rather than competition. The crown of each day's work is a concert, the programme being built round an important choral work, which the choirs have practised during the winter. From it the test-piece has been chosen, and the judging of the choirs fills the morning. The afternoon is spent in rehearsing under a conductor of eminence; and in the evening the singers—usually about 300—join with the orchestra (recruited from the district) and, keyed up to the situation, reach unexpected heights of accomplishment. At the small Hampshire town of Petersfield there is a thirty-year-old festival at which this musical co-operation goes on for four days—children, choirs from villages, small towns and large centres. And Petersfield is by no means alone. At least half a dozen other south-country festivals of the kind could be named.

But perhaps even more remarkable—and certainly more encouraging in its bearings on the future and possibilities of parish church choirs—is the revival of the Diocesan Choral Festival. This is one of the musical happenings that seemed likely to be killed by the war: instead, it is stronger than ever, and better too, both in the choice of music and in the increased attention given to responding, chanting and hymn-singing. Many festivals, indeed, confine themselves to music within the power of a village choir; and at the other end of the scale we see gatherings of town choirs singing anthems and services of a type that would have been beyond the power of the same kind of choir twenty years ago. A few figures, incomplete though they are, will give an idea of the scope and vitality of this movement. The *Musical Times* for 1932 contained reports of over thirty church choir festivals, most of them held in cathedrals. The number of choirs and singers was not always given, but filling in the gaps from our experience of the size of such gatherings, we estimate that in 1932 nearly 600 choirs took part, with a total of about 12,000 singers; and in 1933 the totals were even larger. To these must be added a considerable number of smaller festivals, reports of which did not reach the office of the journal, such as small local gatherings (very important, these, for decentralization must play its part in the movement); nor does the list include any of the numberless Welsh hymn-singing gatherings.

All this activity is of the right heartening sort— village joining with village, town with town, with the cathedral or central large church or chapel as the focal point. The parson of a tiny parish who had brought his little body of singers to a festival for the first time told us that the experience had greatly stimulated his choir. "Hitherto," he said, "they have been difficult to keep together: now they realize that they are an entity, with a real place in an army of church singers."

Can there be any doubt that for all kinds of corporate music-making the omens are good? More and more, people are beginning to realize that the joys of listening are not to be compared with the joys of doing.

Let us again emphasize the need of adequate staffing. This means a great increase in the number of trained leaders. It may be long before Parliament sees the wisdom of spending a modest yearly sum on such an object. Meanwhile the choirmasters of the churches and chapels must form the bulk of the general staff of the vast territorial army of church music makers. Many are good organists, many are enthusiastic ; but the proportion of skilled choir-trainers and conductors is far too small. Here the clergy can and must help (as has been said elsewhere in this book) by making attendance at a choir-training course, or the possession of a choir-training diploma, one of the conditions of holding a post. After all, to do this is merely to apply to the vital matter of choir-training the test that is always applied to organ-playing.

CHAPTER XV

CONCLUSION

IN so endless a matter as this of uniting the duty
called worship with the art called music, our dual
discussion upon it must needs be inconclusive.
Perhaps our best wish will have been attained if readers
are provoked to begin discussion of some of the chief
issues at the point where we leave off.

It is a strange reflection, yet one to which we are both
brought, that in the matter of putting church music
ideals into effect, nearly all is yet to be done—yes,
though devoted men have worked ceaselessly for centuries, with love and ability which we can only revere
and humbly emulate. They have nourished this heavenly
infant-partnership, of worship with music. We all can
but carry on their work and refuse to be discouraged
if it takes our present-day church choirs (of numbers
ranging from four to forty voices) a year's hard practice
to sing even the simplest and most familiar of church
music with such unconscious efficiency that the prayer
itself is really musical, and the music is inherently a
prayer—a carrier of worship, enhanced by being harmonious—that is, made a better vehicle of the spirit
by being purposefully attuned, or at-oned. But to this
end, what is needed on both sides of the equation?
Endless practice to make choral art daily a little
more able to forget itself; and endless devotion to

render the duty-factor in worship more and more unconscious.

In the whole range of church music it is of the essence of the union that the art must grow care-free and the duty grow unconscious. This double need is indeed unsparing ; but wherever enthusiasm reigns, men, women and children always will be found ready to labour unremittingly to this end. Keats has voiced the rapture all can share, when art and duty begin to forget themselves in the sheer happiness of their union :

> " O world as God has made it, all is Beauty !
> And knowing this is Love, and Love is Duty !"

And the Christian artist, musical or otherwise, has his own way of reaching this wonderful position by considering the lilies' glory and not Solomon's. The Christian temper contemplates the natural beauty of melody and of choral harmony with the very same deep and loving regard that our Lord Himself paid to the lilies of the field. This ideal is high, yet easy to comprehend, as high as heaven, yet most homely. The choir that agrees to put fitting Beauty, and only Beauty, into practice has an endless road to traverse, week by week. Taking pains for life is, however, only practical politics for all folk when the goal is seen to be glorious—not by one man here and there, but by a congenial and painstaking team. When this is realized, practices innumerable are felt to be no hardship.

Church music must be a life-hobby to the adult chorister. We can testify from personal experience that for years the boys of one choir gave ten practices a week regularly to prepare for two services a week, and found the effort neither wearing nor adequate. Now that broadcasting is stimulating public discernment and continually raising the standard of church team-work ; and now that the workers of the world are likely to find themselves in possession of an increasing proportion (likely to become an established high proportion) of leisure, it is becoming clear that creative pursuits must increase. We may reasonably believe that there exists no more perfect or more permanent outlet for the inspirited use of creative leisure than that which is offered to all men and women of goodwill in the several orders of music that can be used as the voice of worship.